My passion is and always has been crafting. As my projects became more involved, I came to realize there was a need for innovative products to allow for creativity without limitation. In 2003, my husband, Jeff, and I decided to create a universal die-cut system with die templates that are the most detailed on the market. In 2004, Jeff developed the first incremental die templates to fill the need, not only for me, but also for all avid crafters. They were known as Geometrics and are the inspiration of our famously popular line of Spellbinders™ Nestabilities®.

We created Spellbinders Nestabilities to acknowledge and fulfill customer requests, listening to suggestions from card makers, scrapbookers and other talented artists. These die templates do it all—cut, emboss and stencil. There are no other dies on the market that compare. What a fulfilling business we have developed, creating exquisitely detailed paper-crafting tools for you that delight, inspire and provide value!

Spellbinders™ Nestabilities® Basics & Beyond is a showcase of stunningly detailed paper-craft projects. Included is a chapter focused on techniques used, with an array of options to inspire you to easily create dazzling items for your special moments and obtain more value from your Nestabilities. There are projects for every skill level and for a variety of significant events: birthdays, winter holidays, baby and life moments. I think you'll love the contemporary and fun, sophisticated and elegant, and vintage/shabby chic styles of design in each project-based chapter.

My vision has come to life; my dream has come true, and it is a great pleasure to share these gorgeous projects with you. I am so proud we have assembled a team of the best designers in the industry to show you the limitless possibilities when using Spellbinders Nestabilities. They are talented, gracious and inspiring. I'd like to say a special thank you to my dear friends and mentors, Julie McGuffee and Jean Kievlan, whose steadfast support, encouragement and advice since the inception of Spellbinders has meant the world to me. You are true craft visionaries and an inspiration to us all!

Our goal is to develop paper-crafting products to inspire you to create beautiful, professionally finished projects. Spellbinders' product line is universal, so there are no creative limits. I know you will enjoy this book as much as I do!

Thank you for sharing my vision,

Stacey

Stacey Caron has been scrapbooking and number of years, and her enthusiasm for pc inspires others. She has taught throughout and internationally for retailers, private groups, scrapbook and stamping stores, distributors and sales-rep groups. Prior to establishing Spellbinders, Stacey practiced dentistry for 11 years as a registered dental hygienist. She and her husband, Jeff, have been married for 16 years and have two young sons, Nathan and Justin.

Spellbinders™ Nestabilities® Basics & Beyond

EDITOR Tanya Fox

ART DIRECTOR Brad Snow

PUBLISHING SERVICES DIRECTOR Brenda Gallmeyer

ASSOCIATE EDITOR Brooke Smith

ASSISTANT ART DIRECTOR Nick Pierce

COPY SUPERVISOR Deborah Morgan

COPY EDITORS Emily Carter, Mary O'Donnell

TECHNICAL EDITOR Corene Painter

PHOTOGRAPHY SUPERVISOR Tammy Christian

PHOTO STYLISTS Tammy Liechty, Tammy Steiner

PHOTOGRAPHY Matthew Owen

PRODUCTION ARTIST SUPERVISOR Erin Augsburger

GRAPHIC ARTIST Nicole Gage

PRODUCTION ASSISTANTS Marj Morgan, Judy Neuenschwander

ISBN: 978-1-59635-359-6
Printed in USA
1 2 3 4 5 6 7 8 9

Spellbinders Nestabilities Basics & Beyond is published by DRG, 306 East Parr Road, Berne, IN 46711. Printed in USA. Copyright © 2011 DRG. All rights reserved. This publication may not be reproduced in part or in whole without written permission from the publisher.

RETAIL STORES: If you would like to carry this pattern book or any other DRG publications, visit DRGwholesale.com.

Every effort has been made to ensure that the instructions in this publication are complete and accurate. We cannot, however, take responsibility for human error, typographical mistakes or variations in individual work. Please visit AnniesCustomerCare.com to check for pattern updates.

4 Special Techniques

Baby

Birthday

Mid-Continent Public Library
15616 East Highway 24
Independence, MO 64050

Christmas

Life's Moments

Die Cutting

Tip: Save the die cut from the window for another project!

Cut shapes with Spellbinders™ die templates by creating a die-cutting sandwich.

1. Stack items in the following order: master cut mat; magnetic spacer mat; die template, cutting edge up; card stock; and remaining master cut mat (photo 1).

2. Keeping the sandwich flat and straight, insert it into the die-cutting/embossing machine. Turn the handle until the sandwich exits the other side of the machine (photo 2).

3. Remove the sandwich.

4. Open the sandwich and reveal the die cut (photo 3).

Embossing

To emboss die-cut shapes, create an embossing sandwich with the die-cut shape still placed within the die template.

1. Stack items in the following order: master cut mat; die template, cutting edge up with card stock still in die template; embossing pad; and remaining master cut mat (photo 4).

2. Keeping the sandwich flat and straight, insert it into the die-cutting/embossing machine. Turn the handle until the sandwich exits the other side of the machine.

3. Remove the sandwich.

4. Open the sandwich top and reveal the die-cut/embossed project (photo 5).

Die Cutting Stamped Images

Getting perfect placement to cut images with Spellbinders die templates is so simple!

1. Stamp an image onto paper or card stock.

2. Place die template over stamped area, cutting side down; center die for perfect placement (photo 6).

3. Use repositionable tape to secure die template onto paper or card stock.

4. Run through manual die-cutting machine to cut (photo 7). Follow Embossing instructions to emboss this piece if desired.

Tip: Tape die template to paper on outer edge of die template to avoid damage to stamped image.

Embossing With Impressabilities™ Templates

To emboss with Impressabilities templates, create an embossing sandwich.

1. Stack items in the following order: master cut mat, Impressabilities template, card stock, embossing pad, and remaining master cut mat (photo 8).

2. Keeping the sandwich flat and straight, insert it into the die-cutting/embossing machine. Turn the handle until the sandwich exits the other side of the machine.

3. Remove the sandwich.

4. Open the sandwich to reveal the embossed project (photo 9).

Tip: Die-cut shapes can be embossed with Impressabilities templates. Place die template, cutting edge up, with card stock still in die template in place of the card stock in embossing sandwich in step 1.

Selective Die Cutting

Stretch your creativity in die cutting! Try selective cutting to further customize your crafts.

1. Place die template over a portion of paper, felt or other medium.

2. Secure in place with repositionable tape (photo 10).

3. Run through manual die-cutting machine to create a custom die-cut image (photo 11).

Making a Shaped Card

Why be limited to standard-size cards when you can use Spellbinders die templates to make custom-shaped cards? Follow these easy instructions:

1. Form a top- or side-folded card.

2. Place folded edge of card inside die template cutting line (photo 12).

3. Use repositionable tape to secure die template to card.

4. Run through manual die-cutting machine to create a custom-shaped and embossed card (photo 13).

Making Windows

Whether you want to make a window for a card front or a window in an altered book, the technique is the same. Spellbinders die templates make creating windows easy!

1. Use repositionable tape to secure die template to paper or card stock for perfect placement (photo 14).

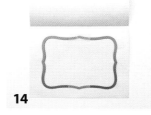

2. Run through manual die-cutting machine (photo 15).

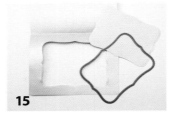

Tip: Save the die cut from the window for another project!

Making Frames

Do you ever want to make the perfect frame but dislike using a craft knife? Spellbinders Nestabilities make creating frames super simple!

1. Choose two die templates in desired shapes.

2. Secure larger die template to paper or card stock with repositionable tape. This will be the outside edge of the frame.

3. Nest smaller die template inside larger die template; secure with repositionable tape. This will make the opening of the frame (photo 16).

4. Run through manual die-cutting machine to create a custom frame (photo 17).

Tip: Don't limit yourself to one shape; mix up Nestabilities to create custom-shaped and -sized frames. Save inside die cut to use on another project.

Using Die Templates As Stencils

To get a great finished look, try this fun technique!

1. Die-cut and emboss paper or card stock with die template.

2. Leave paper or card stock in die template with cutting edge down.

3. Apply ink or chalk to paper through open areas of die template (photo 18).

4. Remove paper or card stock from die template (photo 19).

Tip: Use an airbrush marker system to lightly color embossed areas. Nestabilities allow for an uncolored border around the die cut. Other die templates allow for colored, embossed features, depending on the shapes and images within the die template.

Reverse Stenciling

Add color to die templates to change the look of your die cuts by reverse stenciling! Create colored borders from Nestabilities and colored fields within Shapeabilities® die templates.

1. Apply ink generously to cutting edge of die template (photo 20).

2. Die-cut and emboss as usual.

3. The die cut will be inked in all areas covered by inked die template (photo 21).

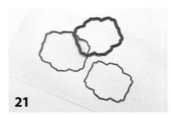

Tip: Use pigment ink for more intense color. Save the negative piece to use on another project.

Pinwheel Technique

1. Die-cut a 3½ x 3½-inch square from card stock using #7 Classic Squares LG die template.

2. Draw diagonal lines on the back of the square die cut. With scissors, cut diagonal lines to within ½ inch of the center point (photo 22).

3. Bring lower right corner of each formed triangle to center of square. Punch a hole through center, going through all layers. Insert a brad to secure corners to center (photo 23).

Tip: Vary the size of your pinwheel by using different sizes of square Spellbinders Nestabilities.

Tissue-Paper Carnations

What a quick and clever way to make a colorful bouquet of tissue-paper carnations!

1. Fold a large sheet of tissue paper in half; continue folding until you have 12–16 layers of tissue paper.

2. Die-cut folded tissue paper using a circular die such as Classic Scalloped Circles (photo 24).

3. Punch two small holes in center; thread floss or string through holes and tie a double knot; trim ends to ¼ inch (photo 25).

4. Start to gather each piece of tissue towards center on opposite side of knot (photo 26).

5. Once all layers are gathered, start pulling layers down one by one—starting with outside layer—to form carnation flower shape (photo 27).

Tips: Use different sizes of Spellbinders circular dies to create small and large flowers.

Use different colors of tissue together to make multicolored flowers.

Spirit of Christmas Box-Top Technique

1. Using 4-inch (#6) Petite Scalloped Circle LG die template, die-cut/emboss a scalloped circle from white card stock; set aside. Die-cut/emboss four circles from red card stock using 3¾-inch (#7) Standard Circles LG die template.

2. For each circle, mountain-fold in half, unfold, pivot 90 degrees, and then mountain-fold again and unfold, pivot 45 degrees, valley-fold and then unfold (photo 28).

3. Fold-in circle on both sides along the valley fold, resulting in pie-shaped piece equal to ¼ of the original circle's size (photo 29).

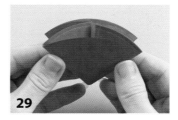

4. Measure ½ inch in from side of top layer of one pie-shaped piece. Score line and fold edge down as shown (photo 30).

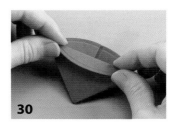

5. Adhere all four pie-shaped pieces to scalloped circle (photo 31).

Making a Tree

1. Using Spellbinders Classic Scalloped Circles LG die templates, die-cut a 2⅛-inch (#2), 3⅛-inch (#4) and 4⅛-inch (#6) scalloped circle from both card stock and scrap paper.

2. Fold each scrap-paper scalloped circle in half, then in half again (photo 32).

3. Unfold and lay scalloped circles over corresponding card-stock circles. Scissor-cut along one creased line, stopping at the center of the circles (photo 33).

4. Create cone shapes from card-stock scalloped circles by overlapping five scallops at cut edges (photo 34).

5. Adhere overlapping scalloped ends together; pierce a hole through last overlapping scallop and insert a brad (photo 35).

6. Repeat with remaining scalloped circles.

7. Cut off center top of the cones large enough to fit over a wooden dowel (photo 36).

8. Cut a straw into three pieces, 1-inch, ¾-inch and ½-inch. From large to small, slide a piece of straw onto wooden dowel followed by a scalloped cone (photo 37).

Tip: *Try Petite or Big Scalloped Circles for a variation on this project!*

Pyramid-Image Technique

It's easy to get a pyramid effect with Spellbinders Nestabilities!

1. Print or stamp six copies of an image onto cream card stock. Place smallest die template (sample uses Labels Eleven) centered onto one image, cutting side facedown; secure die template with removable tape (photo 38). Die-cut the image.

2. Align the die-cut image on top of an intact image. Center the next largest die template over the intact image and secure with removable tape (photo 39). Die-cut image. Repeat this process with remaining images, increasing the size of die template with each die-cut.

3. Using the largest die-cut image as a base, center and layer the die cuts, using dimensional foam tape (photo 40).

Dimensional Flowers

1. Using 2-inch (#3) Blossom die template, die-cut and emboss three flowers from paper.

2. Cut a slit in one flower, cut out one petal from second flower, and cut out two petals from third flower (photo 41).

3. Overlap cut edges of each flower and glue to form three cone shapes. Roll the cutout one-petal piece from step 2 into a cylinder shape; glue ends together to secure. Repeat with the cutout two-petal piece from step 2 (photo 42).

4. Shape petals on each cone-shaped flower (photo 43).

5. Nest layers inside of each other, largest to smallest, using two- and one-petal cylinders for center; glue layers together (photo 44). **Note:** *If needed, cut off bottom of portions of cylinders to make them fit properly.*

Making a Rose

1. Die-cut two of each Deckled Rectangles LG die templates #1–#5 (#1 is the smallest) from red card stock, for a total of ten deckled rectangles.

2. Start to form a rose by spraying the two smallest deckled rectangle die cuts with Glimmer Mist. Wrap die-cut pieces around a wooden floral pick, one piece at a time. Mold each die cut into a petal shape and secure with wire (photo 45).

3. Repeat with the second smallest die cuts, wrapping these die cuts around the smallest die cuts. Spray Glimmer Mist as needed to mold into rose-petal shapes. Continue working from smallest to largest die cuts to add layers for rose (photo 46).

4. Attach finished rose to floral stem with floral tape (photo 47). Spray finished rose with Glimmer Mist.

Baby Shower Ensemble

DESIGNS BY **DEBBIE SEYER**

Baby Bibs

Using 4-inch (#7) Big Scalloped Circles LG die template, die-cut/emboss two scalloped circles from aqua card stock and two from peach card stock.

Using 3¼-inch (#6) Standard Circles LG die template, die-cut/emboss four circles from white card stock. Adhere a white circle centered to each scalloped circle.

Following Selective Die Cutting instructions on page 5, position Standard Classic Ovals LG 3 x 2¼-inch (#4) die template on top of a layered circle with repositionable tape; die-cut/emboss to form a baby-bib shape. Repeat with remaining scalloped circles.

Stamp four different baby sentiments onto white card stock leaving space between each. Referring to Die Cutting Stamped Images instructions on page 4, die-cut/emboss all sentiments using 2¼ x 1⅛-inch (#1) Petite Ovals LG die template.

Using 1½ x 2½-inch (#2) Petite Scalloped Ovals SM die template, die-cut/emboss two scalloped ovals from aqua card stock and two scalloped ovals from peach card stock. Adhere a sentiment oval to each scalloped oval. Adhere layered ovals to baby bibs as shown.

Cut both 24-inch lengths of ribbon in half. Tie a bow with each piece of ribbon forming four bows. Referring to photo, pierce a hole through both sides of each bib and attach ribbons to bibs with brads.

Sources: *Colored card stock and ribbons from Papertrey Ink; white card stock from Gina K. Designs; brads from Stampin' Up!; die templates from Spellbinders™ Paper Arts.*

Materials

- Card stock: aqua, peach, white
- Practically Perfect stamp set
- Black dye ink pad
- 24 inches each ½-inch-wide satin ribbon: aqua, peach
- 8 white brads
- Nestabilities® die templates: Big Scalloped Circles LG (#S4-249), Standard Circles LG (#S4-114), Classic Ovals LG (#S4-110), Petite Ovals LG (#S4-138), Petite Scalloped Ovals SM (#S4-141),
- Manual die-cutting and embossing machine
- Paper piercer
- Repositionable tape
- Paper adhesive

Did You Know?

You can create garland and pennants with Nestabilities.

We can't wait *to meet you*

Our little **miracle**

Sweet child **of mine**

A baby is a bit of *stardust* blown from the *hand of God.*

Let's Welcome The New Baby
When: July 4, 2010
Where: Our House
Time: 2:00 p.m.
Regrets Only: 123-345-6789

Special delivery

Welcome **baby**

Welcome **baby**

Materials

- Card stock: aqua, peach, white
- Practically Perfect stamp set
- Black dye ink pad
- Markers
- Black fine-tip marker
- 12 inches ½-inch-wide aqua or peach satin ribbon
- Nestabilities die templates: Big Scalloped Circles LG (#S4-249), Big Scalloped Circles SM (#S4-250), Standard Circles SM (#S4-116), Big Scalloped Ovals SM (#S4-252), Classic Ovals LG (#S4-110)
- Manual die-cutting and embossing machine
- ½-inch slot punch
- Adhesive foam dots
- Paper adhesive
- Computer with printer (optional)

Special Delivery Baby-Shower Invitation

Form a 5½ x 4¼-inch top-folded card from aqua or peach card stock. Referring to Making a Shaped Card instructions on page 5, position a 4⅛ x 4⅛-inch (#7) Big Scalloped Circle LG die template onto card to die-cut/emboss a scalloped circle card.

Using 3¼-inch (#6) Big Scalloped Circles SM die template, die-cut/emboss two scalloped circles from peach or aqua card stock; set one aside. Stamp little girl or little boy bunny onto white card stock; color with markers. Referring to Die Cutting Stamped Images instructions on page 4, using 3-inch (#6) Standard Circles SM die template, die-cut/emboss image.

Adhere stamped circle to scalloped circle. Using slot punch, punch a slot to the left and right of bunny. Thread desired color of ribbon through slots as shown; tie knot on right side, trim ends. Adhere to card front as shown.

Stamp "Special Delivery" onto white card stock. In the same manner as before, die-cut/emboss sentiment using 1 x ¾-inch (#1) Classic Ovals LG die template.

Using 1⅛ x ⅞-inch (#1) Big Scalloped Ovals SM die template, die-cut/emboss a scalloped oval from peach or aqua card stock. Adhere sentiment oval to scalloped oval. Attach to card front using foam dots as shown.

Hand-print, or use a computer to generate, baby-shower information onto white card stock. Using 3-inch (#6) Standard Circles SM die template, die-cut/emboss sentiment. Adhere to set-aside scalloped circle. Adhere inside card.

Sources: *Colored card stock and ribbon from Papertrey Ink; white card stock from Gina K. Designs; Copic markers from Imagination International Inc.; die templates from Spellbinders™ Paper Arts.*

Let's Welcome The New Baby
When: July 4, 2010
Where: Our House
Time: 2:00 p.m.
Regrets Only: 123-345-6789

Did You Know?

You can create shaped cards with Nestabilities.

Welcome Baby Table Favors

Using Labels Ten die template, die-cut/emboss a 2 x 1¼-inch (#1) label from aqua and peach card stock. Die-cut/emboss a 2⅞ x 1⅞-inch (#2) label from peach and aqua card stock. Adhere smaller labels centered to larger labels.

Stamp "Welcome baby" twice onto white card stock. Following Die Cutting Stamped Images instructions on page 4, die-cut/emboss sentiments using 1¾ x 1¼-inch (#2) Classic Ovals LG die template. Layer and adhere labels as shown.

Cut ribbon into two 12-inch lengths. Tie a bow with one 12-inch length, leaving a 2-inch tail on each side. Repeat with other 12-inch ribbon. Adhere ribbons to container lids using double-sided adhesive. ▣

Sources: *Colored card stock and ribbon from Papertrey Ink; white card stock from Gina K. Designs; die templates from Spellbinders™ Paper Arts.*

Materials

- Card stock: aqua, peach, white
- Plastic storage jars
- Practically Perfect stamp set
- Black dye ink pad
- 24 inches ½-inch-wide aqua or peach satin ribbon
- Nestabilities die templates: Labels Ten (#S5-022); Classic Ovals LG (#S4-110)
- Manual die-cutting and embossing machine
- Double-sided adhesive
- Paper adhesive

Vintage Baby

DESIGNS BY **HOLLY SIMONI**

Materials

- Card stock: pink, cream
- Ducks in a Row Pat-a-Cake double-sided printed paper
- Ducks in a Row Ducks Words stickers
- Just a Note Borders & Centers stamp set
- Chalk ink pads: brown, pink
- Pink ribbons: 3½ inches ¼-inch-wide scalloped velvet, 14 inches 1-inch-wide sheer
- White eyelet
- Crystal stickpin
- Nestabilities® die templates: Lacey Squares (#S4-295), Beaded Circles (#S4-292)
- Manual die-cutting and embossing machine
- ⅛-inch hole punch
- Eyelet-setting tool
- Craft sponge
- Adhesive foam squares
- Tacky glue
- Paper adhesive

"B" Is for Baby Card

Using Lacey Squares die template, die-cut/emboss a 4¼ x 4¼-inch (#5) square and a 2½ x 2½-inch (#3) square from printed paper; die-cut/emboss a 3¼ x 3¼-inch (#4) square from pink card stock. Ink edges of printed-paper squares brown.

Adhere pink square to center of largest printed-paper square. Attach baby definition sticker to center of smallest printed-paper square. Using foam squares, attach smallest printed-paper square to layered squares.

Adhere velvet ribbon to center of sheer ribbon using tacky glue. Wrap layered ribbon around card; tie knot on right side; trim ends.

Using pink ink, stamp Celebrate image onto cream card stock. Following Die Cutting Stamped Images instructions on page 4, die-cut/emboss stamped area using 2⅞-inch (#3) Beaded Circles die template.

Punch a hole through top of die-cut circle; set eyelet in hole. Place stickpin through eyelet. Attach to lower right corner of card front using foam squares.

Sources: *Card stock from WorldWin Papers; printed papers from October Afternoon; stamp set from JustRite; ink pads from Clearsnap Inc.; ribbons from Maya Road; stickpin from Making Memories; die templates from Spellbinders™ Paper Arts.*

Did You Know?

You can make your own journaling tags with Nestabilities.

Our Miracle Has Arrived Mini Album

Using 5⅛ x 3½-inch (#6) Labels Seventeen die template, die-cut/emboss eight labels from a variety of printed papers. Adhere labels together to form four album pages. Ink edges of pages with a variety of inks, as desired.

For album cover, create a frame using This Little Piggy paper and 5⅛ x 3½-inch (#6) and 4⅜ x 3-inch (#5) Labels Seventeen die templates following the Making Frames instructions on page 6. Ink edges brown. Using foam squares, attach frame to album page that you want to be the album's cover.

Die-cut/emboss a 3 x 2-inch (#3) label from This Little Piggy paper; ink edges brown. Die-cut/emboss a 2¼ x 1½-inch (#2) label from lined journaling card; ink edges brown. Pierce two holes ¾ inch apart along bottom of lined label; insert a stickpin through holes.

Trim "Our miracle has arrived" sticker down to a 1¼ x ¾-inch rectangle; attach to lined label. Using tacky glue, attach edges of lined label to printed-paper label as shown, letting lined label curve slightly in middle. Using foam squares, attach label to center of album cover.

Using 1¾-inch (#2) Beaded Circles die template, die-cut/emboss three beaded circles from cream card stock. Ink edges of beaded circles with a variety of inks as desired. Attach a round word sticker to each beaded circle.

Embellish each page of album as desired, using die cuts, die-cut journaling cards, stickers, baby photos and stickpins.

Lay album pages on top of each other. Using hole punch, punch two holes through left side of pages as shown. Cut ribbon into two 5-inch lengths. Thread a length of ribbon through one set of holes; tie knot; trim ends. Repeat with second length of ribbon and second set of holes.

Sources: *Card stock from WorldWin Papers; printed papers, journal cards and stickers from October Afternoon; ink pads from Clearsnap Inc.; ribbons from Maya Road; stickpins from Making Memories; die templates from Spellbinders™ Paper Arts.*

Materials

- Cream card stock
- Ducks in a Row double-sided printed papers: Pat-a-Cake, Lullaby, Sleep Tight, Peek-a-Boo, This Little Piggy
- Report Card Story Hour double-sided printed paper
- Ducks in a Row Ducks Journal Cards
- Ducks in a Row Ducks Words stickers
- Baby photos (optional)
- Chalk ink pads: turquoise, brown, black, pink, lime green
- 10 inches 1-inch-wide pink sheer ribbon
- 6 crystal stickpins
- Nestabilities die templates: Labels Seventeen (#S5-025), Beaded Circles (#S4-292)
- Manual die-cutting and embossing machine
- ³⁄₁₆-inch hole punch
- Paper piercer
- Adhesive foam squares
- Tacky glue
- Paper adhesive

Did You Know?

You can leave paper in your Spellbinders die template and stencil through the die template with Glimmer Mist, ink, chalk or markers.

Materials

- White gift box
- Card stock: cream, yellow, pink
- Ducks in a Row double-sided printed papers: Pat-a-Cake, Sleep Tight, This Little Piggy, Splish Splash
- Ducks in a Row Ducks Words stickers
- Chalk ink pads: brown, black
- Black fine-tip marker
- Pink ribbons: approximately 21 inches ¼-inch-wide scalloped velvet, approximately 29 inches 1-inch-wide sheer
- Crystal stickpin
- 2 blue flat-back acrylic stones
- Nestabilities die templates: Standard Circles LG (#S4-114), Beaded Circles (#S4-292)
- Manual die-cutting and embossing machine
- Craft sponge
- Adhesive foam squares
- Tacky glue
- Paper adhesive

Keepsake Box

Cover outer edges of gift-box lid and bottom with printed papers as desired; ink edges brown. Cut a piece of sheer ribbon long enough to wrap around box; wrap ribbon around box bottom and adhere. Adhere velvet ribbon over sheer ribbon.

Using a 4¼-inch (#4) Beaded Circles die template, die-cut/emboss a beaded circle from cream card stock. Using die template as a stencil, ink raised areas of beaded circle with craft sponge and brown ink, as instructed in Using Die Templates As Stencils instructions on page 6. Adhere beaded circle to top of box. Cut a length of sheer ribbon long enough to fit across width of box lid with extra to wrap inside; wrap ribbon across lid and secure ends inside. Adhere a length of velvet ribbon over sheer ribbon with tacky glue; secure ends inside lid.

Die-cut/emboss a 2⅞-inch (#3) beaded circle from Sleep Tight paper and a 1¾-inch (#2) beaded circle from yellow card stock. In the same manner as before, ink printed-paper circle with black ink; ink yellow circle with brown ink. Set aside.

Using 3¼-inch (#6) Standard Circles LG die template, die-cut/emboss a circle from pink card stock. Die-cut/emboss a 1⅞-inch (#3) circle from yellow card stock.

Layer and adhere all die-cut pieces as shown, using foam squares to "pop up" layers as desired. Attach a round "Date:" sticker to center of top die cut. Attach "Baby's First" sticker with hand-printed message as shown. Cut a duckling from Splish Splash paper; adhere to box as shown.

Adhere an acrylic stone onto ribbon on either side of die cuts. Tie a bow with sheer ribbon; trim ends. Adhere to box lid as shown. Embellish with stickpin. ■

Sources: *Card stock from WorldWin Papers; printed papers and stickers from October Afternoon; ink pads from Clearsnap Inc.; ribbons from Maya Road; stickpin from Making Memories; Tear Drops acrylic stones from The Robin's Nest; die templates from Spellbinders™ Paper Arts.*

Baby Celebration

DESIGNS BY **JULIE OVERBY**

Congrats On Your New Baby Card

Project note: Ink all edges of cut pieces light brown unless instructed otherwise.

Form a 6 x 6-inch top-folded card from kraft card stock. Die-cut bottom edge of card front using Fair Isle die template. Ink edges of card front pink and brown.

Cut a 5½ x 5½-inch piece from Houndstooth paper; distress edges. Adhere to card front as shown.

Using 5 x 5-inch (#3) Grand Squares die template and Grand Calibur die-cutting machine, die-cut a square from Honey Bunch paper; adhere to card front.

Adhere a 5 x 1-inch piece of Decorative Edge card stock to bottom edge of a 5 x 2-inch piece of Floral paper as shown. Cut a 5 x ¾-inch piece of felt, die-cut bottom edge with Grand Scalloped Squares die template; do not ink edges. Adhere felt strip to bottom edge of layered paper panel. Cut a 5 x ½-inch strip from yellow grid paper; adhere to bottom edge of paper panel as shown. Adhere panel 1½ inches above bottom edge. Zigzag-stitch top and bottom edge of Floral paper piece.

Using Labels Fourteen die template, die-cut/emboss a 1¾ x 3⅝-inch (#3) label from Honey Bunch paper and 2⅜ x 3⅝-inch (#4) labels from Houndstooth and Honey Bunch papers. Adhere Honey Bunch label to Houndstooth label as shown.

Adhere smallest label to white card stock; trim a small border. Sponge inside edges of label pink. Adhere baby in basket cotton image to label as shown. Using brown ink, stamp sentiment below baby. Using foam squares, attach stamped label to larger label. Adhere to card front as shown.

Tie bows with both colors of seam binding or ribbon; layer and adhere to card front as shown. Thread button with white string; tie bow in front. Adhere to center of bows. Embellish bows with two stickpins; secure with foam square. Attach stickers to card front as shown to spell "baby."

Sources: *Kraft card stock from WorldWin Papers; Fresh Print Clothesline Decorative Edge card stock from Little Yellow Bicycle/The C-Thru Ruler Co.; Lush Pink printed papers from My Mind's Eye; Sweet Cakes printed paper from Pink Paislee; chipboard stickers from American Crafts Inc.; stamp set from Fiskars; ink pads from Clearsnap Inc. and Tsukineko LLC; pearl stickpins from Maya Road; button from Jenni Bowlin Studio; Baby Boy Homespun Cotton Scraps from Crafty Secrets Publications; die templates and Grand Calibur™ machine from Spellbinders™ Paper Arts.*

Did You Know?

You can cut thin cotton fabric with Spellbinders die templates.

Materials

- Card stock: kraft, white
- Printed card stock: yellow grid, Fresh Print Clothesline Decorative Edge
- Double-sided printed papers: Lush Pink Houndstooth, Lush Pink Floral, Sweet Cakes Honey Bunch
- White felt
- Pink chipboard alphabet stickers
- Round of Applause stamp set
- Chalk ink pads: light brown, pink
- 2 white pearl stickpins
- Pink button
- 8 inches ½-inch-wide seam binding or ribbon: pink, yellow
- White string
- Baby Boy Homespun Cotton Scraps
- Labels Fourteen Nestabilities® die template (#S4-290)
- Grand Nestabilities® die templates: Squares (#LF-126), Scalloped Squares (#LF-127)
- Fair Isle Borderabilities® Petite die template (#S4-244)
- Grand Calibur™ manual die-cutting and embossing machine
- Sandpaper
- Craft sponge
- Sewing machine with white thread
- Adhesive foam squares
- Adhesive dots
- Instant-dry paper glue

congrats on your
new

baby

it's
a
baby
shower

Baby Shower Invitation

Project note: *Ink all edges of cut pieces light brown unless instructed otherwise.*

Form a 4 x 6½-inch side-folded card from pink card stock. Following Making a Shaped Card instructions on page 5, die-cut/emboss card using 3⅞ x 6-inch (#2) Grand Labels Four die template.

Using 3⅞ x 6-inch (#2) Grand Labels Four die template, die-cut/emboss labels from Floral and Honey Bunch papers. Cut 1½ inches from top and bottom of Honey Bunch label. Cut 1¾ inches from top and bottom of Floral label. Adhere Floral label to Honey Bunch label as shown. Adhere to card front aligning right edge; trim left edge to fit card front. Zigzag-stitch top edge of Floral label. Adhere decorative ribbon to bottom of Floral label as shown.

Using Labels Eleven die template, die-cut/emboss a 2½ x 3½-inch (#5) label from Houndstooth paper and a 2⅛ x 2⅞-inch (#4) label from Honey Bunch paper. Adhere Houndstooth label to white card stock as shown; trim a small border. Adhere Honey Bunch label to Houndstooth label. Attach alphabet stickers to label as shown. Decorate with three pearls. Using foam squares, attach to card front ½ inch above bottom edge.

Ink two chipboard safety pins pink, apply glitter with paper glue. Let dry completely. Slide safety pins onto jute twine; tie a knot. Trim ends. Adhere to top of card front as shown.

Cut seam binding or ribbon in half; tie bows with each piece. Layer and adhere bows to card front as shown. Thread button with white string; tie knot on back. Trim ends. Adhere to center of layered bows.

Sources: *Card stock from Bazzill Basics Paper Inc. and WorldWin Papers; Lush Pink printed papers from My Mind's Eye; Sweet Cakes printed paper from Pink Paislee; chipboard set from Maya Road; alphabet stickers from Cosmo Cricket; ink pads from Clearsnap Inc. and Tsukineko LLC; die templates and Grand Calibur machine from Spellbinders™ Paper Arts.*

Materials

- Card stock: pink, kraft, white
- Double-sided printed papers: Lush Pink Houndstooth, Lush Pink Floral, Lush Pink Finish, Sweet Cakes Honey Bunch
- Sew Cute Mini Chipboard Set
- Small brown alphabet stickers
- Chalk ink pads: light brown, pink
- Clear iridescent glitter
- White pearl button
- 3 cream small self-adhesive pearls
- 16 inches ½-inch-wide yellow seam binding or ribbon
- 3¾ inches ½-inch-wide white decorative ribbon
- White string
- Jute twine
- Labels Eleven Nestabilities die templates (#S4-246)
- Grand Nestabilities die templates: Labels Four (#LF-190), Scalloped Squares (#LF-127)
- Grand Calibur manual die-cutting and embossing machine
- Craft sponge
- Sewing machine with white thread
- Adhesive foam square
- Adhesive dots
- Instant-dry paper glue

Baby Bootie Party Favors

Project note: *Baby bootie template is available at www.kaisercraft.net/pdfs/paper-craft/Booties.pdf.*

Use computer to print baby bootie template onto printer paper. Cut out both pieces of pattern to use as a template. Trace both pieces for bootie onto Houndstooth printed paper; trace bootie sole onto cardboard. Cut out all pieces and assemble according to designer's instructions, adhering cardboard soles to bottoms of printed-paper booties.

Following Reverse Stenciling instructions on page 6, ink edges of ⅝-inch (#1) Dahlia die template pink and die-cut/emboss flower from Honey Bunch paper. Repeat three times, reinking die template before each die cut.

Ink edges of 1¼-inch (#2) Dahlia die template pink; die-cut/emboss flower from Honey Bunch paper. Repeat, reinking die template before second die cut.

Using foam squares, attach a small die-cut flower to each larger die-cut flower. Attach a medium pearl to center of each layered flower. Adhere a layered flower to each baby bootie as shown.

Attach a small pearl to center of each remaining small flower. Using an adhesive dot, adhere a small flower to front of each baby bootie, connecting bootie straps together.

Adhere a 5-inch length of pompom trim to each bootie as shown. Attach two small pearls to front center of each bootie.

Cut two 1½ x 3½-inch pieces from crepe paper. Fold each piece in half lengthwise. Adhere a folded crepe-paper piece to back of each bootie.

In the same manner as before, ink edges of 2¼ x ½-inch Double Ended Tag die template; die-cut/emboss a tag from Honey Bunch paper. Cut ½ inch from each end of tag. Adhere end pieces with holes to top edge of crepe paper on back of each bootie.

Cut 20-inch length of pink seam binding or ribbon in half to create two 10-inch lengths. Tie each piece in a bow and adhere to back of each bootie as shown.

Fill two pieces of netting with candy. To close each piece, bring ends of netting together; wrap string around netting just above candies; tie bow and trim ends. Place candy favors inside booties.

Sources: *Lush Pink printed paper from My Mind's Eye; Sweet Cakes printed paper from Pink Paislee; ink pads from Clearsnap Inc. and Tsukineko LLC; pompom trim from Maya Road; baby bootie template and pearls from Kaisercraft; die templates from Spellbinders™ Paper Arts.*

Materials

- Double-sided printed papers: Lush Pink Houndstooth, Sweet Cakes Honey Bunch
- Cream crepe paper
- Cardboard
- Pink netting
- Chalk ink pads: light brown, pink
- 10 inches ⅜-inch-wide cream pompom trim
- 20 inches ½-inch-wide pink seam binding or ribbon
- String
- Cream self-adhesive pearls: 6 small, 2 medium
- Candy
- Dahlia Nestabilities die templates (#S4-191)
- Double Ended Tags Shapeabilities® die templates (#S3-149)
- Manual die-cutting and embossing machine
- Baby bootie template
- Craft sponge
- Adhesive foam squares
- Adhesive dots
- Paper adhesive
- Instant-dry paper glue
- Computer, printer and printer paper

Retro Birthday

DESIGNS BY **KIMBERLY CRAWFORD**

Materials

- Card stock: gray, orange, aqua, purple, mustard yellow, teal, off-white
- Joy Ride double-sided printed papers: Are We There Yet, Round-A-Bout
- Birthday Messages stamp set
- Watermark ink pad
- White embossing powder
- Standard Circles LG Nestabilities® die templates (#S4-114)
- Manual die-cutting and embossing machine
- Embossing heat tool
- Adhesive foam squares
- Paper adhesive

Happy Birthday Card

Form a 4¼ x5½-inch top-folded card from gray card stock.

Using Standard Circles LG die template, die-cut 1⅜-inch (#2) circle from purple, orange and teal card stock for a total of three circles. Following Making Frames instructions on page 6, use 1⅜-inch (#2) and ⅞-inch (#1) die templates to die-cut/emboss three circle frames from off-white card stock.

Die-cut a 1⅞-inch (#3) circle from mustard yellow card stock and teal card stock. In the same manner as before, create two frames for these circles from off-white card stock using 1⅞-inch (#3) and 1⅜-inch (#2) die templates.

Die-cut a 2⅜-inch (#4) circle from aqua card stock. In the same manner as before, create a frame for this circle from off-white card stock using 2⅜-inch (#4) and 1⅞-inch (#3) die templates.

Adhere circle frames to corresponding circles. Adhere circles randomly to card front, allowing some to run off edges. Trim edges of circles so they align with edges of card.

Adhere a 4¼ x 1¼-inch strip of orange card stock to card front, 1 inch above bottom edge. Adhere a 4¼ x 1-inch piece of Are We There Yet paper over orange strip. Cut a 4¼ x ¾-inch strip of Round-A-Bout paper. Using watermark ink, stamp "Happy Birthday" onto strip as shown. Sprinkle with white embossing powder and heat-emboss using embossing heat tool. Adhere to card front as shown.

Cut a number from Are We There Yet paper. Using foam squares, attach number to card front.

Sources: Colored card stock from Core'dinations; off-white card stock from Papertrey Ink; printed papers from Cosmo Cricket; stamp set from Hero Arts; ink pad from Tsukineko LLC; die templates from Spellbinders™ Paper Arts.

Materials

- Card stock: gray, aqua, off-white
- Birthday Messages stamp set
- Black dye ink pad
- Silver mini brad
- Sucker stick
- Nestabilities die templates: Standard Circles LG (#S4-114), Classic Squares LG (#S4-126)
- Manual die-cutting and embossing machine
- Paper piercer
- Large adhesive foam squares
- Tacky glue
- Paper adhesive

Cupcake Pinwheel

Using a 3½ x 3½-inch (#7) Classic Squares LG die template, and gray card stock, create a pinwheel following Pinwheel Technique instructions on page 6.

Using Standard Circles LG die template, die-cut 1⅜-inch (#2) circle from aqua card stock. Following Making Frames instructions on page 6, use 1⅜-inch (#2) and ⅞-inch (#1) die templates to die-cut/emboss a circle frame from off-white card stock. Adhere frame over aqua circle. Using black ink, stamp sentiment onto framed circle.

Using tacky glue, adhere sucker stick to back of circle ½ inch from bottom edge. Attach two layers of foam squares to back of circle just above sucker stick; attach top foam square to brad on pinwheel.

Sources: Colored card stock from Core'dinations; off-white card stock from Papertrey Ink; stamp set from Hero Arts; die templates from Spellbinders™ Paper Arts.

{ wishing you a
one-of-a-kind
BIRTHDAY }

123

9

SEIZE
the
CAKE

Happy Birthday

CORAL

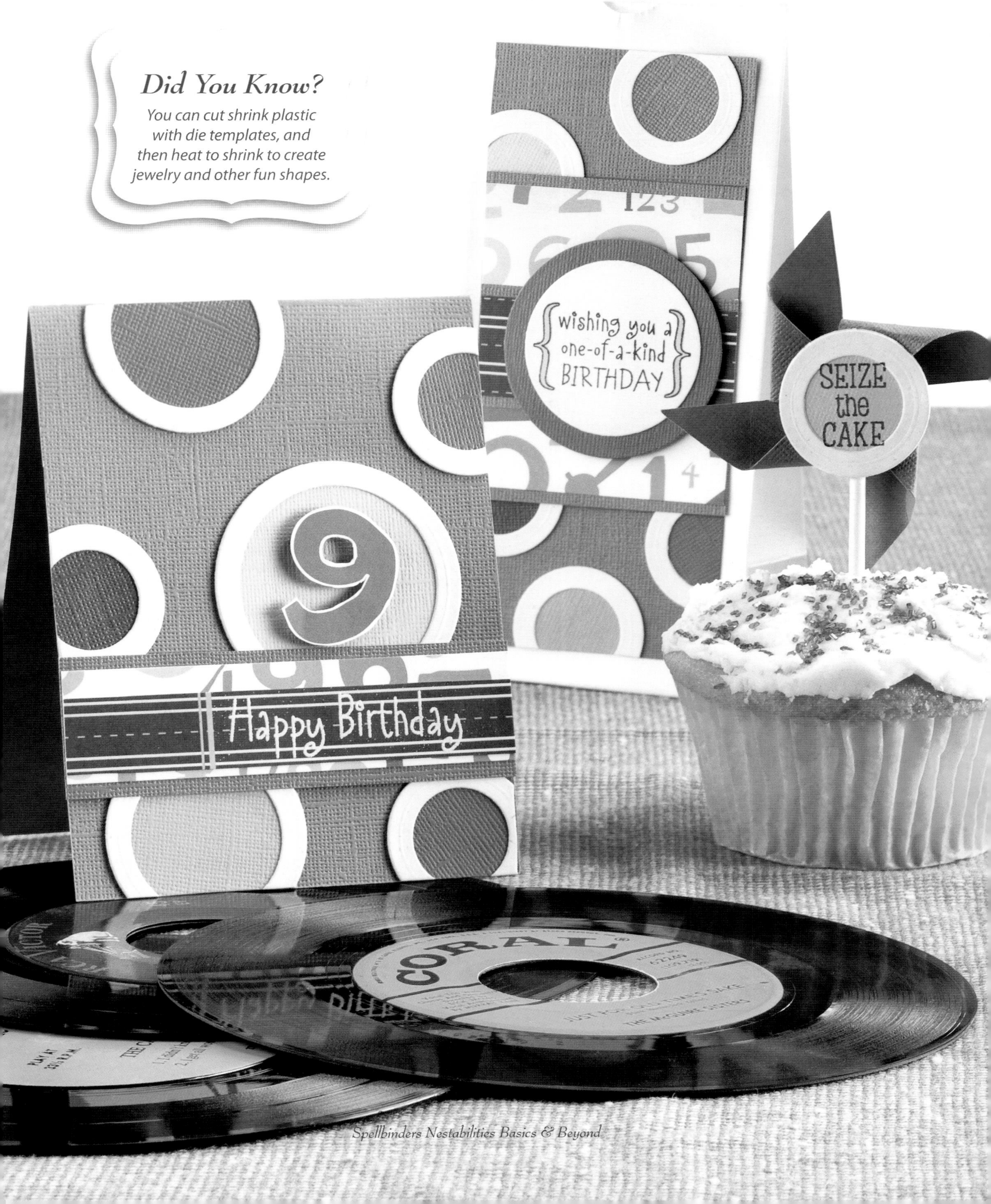

Happy Birthday Treat Bag

Using Standard Circles LG die template, die-cut 1⅜-inch (#2) circle from orange, aqua, purple, mustard yellow and teal card stock for a total of five circles. Following Making Frames instructions on page 6, use 1⅜-inch (#2) and ⅞-inch (#1) die templates to die-cut five circle frames from off-white card stock. Adhere circle frames to card-stock circles.

Cut a 2¾ x 6½-inch piece from gray card stock; adhere framed circles to gray panel as shown. Trim edges of circles so they align with panel edges.

Cut a 2¾ x 3½-inch piece from orange card stock; adhere centered to gray panel. Adhere a 2¾ x 3¼-inch piece of Are We There Yet paper to orange piece. Adhere a 2¾ x 1-inch strip of Round-A-Bout paper to a 2¾ x 1¼-inch strip of orange card stock. Adhere to Are We There Yet paper piece.

Die-cut/emboss 2⅜-inch (#4) circle from teal card stock. Stamp sentiment onto off-white card stock; color with marker as shown. Following Die Cutting Stamped Images instructions on page 4, die-cut sentiment using 1⅞-inch (#3) circle die template. Adhere sentiment circle to teal circle. Using foam squares, attach circle to center of gray panel. Adhere gray panel to front of coffee bag. ■

Sources: Colored card stock from Core'dinations; off-white card stock from Papertrey Ink; printed papers from Cosmo Cricket; coffee bag from Pink Persimmon; stamp set from Hero Arts; Copic marker from Imagination International Inc.; die templates from Spellbinders™ Paper Arts.

Materials

- Card stock: gray, orange, aqua, purple, mustard yellow, teal, off-white
- Joy Ride double-sided printed papers: Are We There Yet, Round-A-Bout
- Small white coffee bag
- Birthday Messages stamp set
- Black dye ink pad
- Yellow marker
- Standard Circles LG Nestabilities die templates (#S4-114)
- Manual die-cutting and embossing machine
- Embossing heat tool
- Adhesive foam squares
- Paper adhesive

Did You Know?

Spellbinders die templates are universal and can be used in other die-cutting machines.

Birds & Blossoms Birthday

DESIGNS BY **LINDA DUKE**

Project notes: Ink edges of all die-cut paper pieces light brown. Use cream thread unless otherwise directed.

Happy Birthday Card

Form a 6⅛ x 6⅛-inch top-folded card from kraft card stock. Adhere a 6⅛ x 6⅛-inch piece of dark cream card stock to card front.

Cut a 6 x 6-inch square from script printed paper; machine-stitch around edges.

Using Long Classic Scalloped Rectangles LG die template, die-cut/emboss a 2⅝ x 5¼-inch (#4) scalloped rectangle from light green printed paper and a 6¼ x 3⅛-inch (#5) scalloped rectangle from dark cream printed paper. Cut ¾ inch from one short edge of dark cream scalloped rectangle. Machine-stitch along long edges. Using foam dots, attach rectangle to 6 x 6-inch printed paper square ⅝ inch above bottom edge, aligning cut edge with right edge of paper.

Cut ¼ inch from one short edge of light green scalloped rectangle. Machine-stitch along long edges. Using foam dots, attach to printed-paper square ½ inch from left edge aligning cut edge with top edge of paper.

Wrap lace trim over light green scalloped rectangle as shown; secure ends to back. Adhere panel to card front.

Using Long Classic Rectangles LG die template, die-cut a 4 x 1⅞-inch (#3) rectangle from felt. Die-cut a slightly smaller rectangle from Birds & Blossoms image. Layer and adhere bird and felt rectangles to card front as shown.

Paint chipboard scroll with crackle paint; let dry completely. Embellish scroll with light green glitter glue; let dry completely. Adhere to card front as shown.

Cut a 4⅜ x ⅝-inch strip from cream striped paper; V-notch both ends. Using dark brown ink, stamp "Happy Birthday" onto strip. Adhere to card front as shown, applying glue to ends of strip only.

Following Tissue-Paper Carnations instructions on page 7, form a flower out of white tissue paper; spray with Glitter Mist; let dry. Apply light brown ink and iridescent glitter glue to edges of flower.

Cut silk ribbon into three pieces, varying lengths.

Materials

- Card stock: kraft, dark cream
- Classic Double-Sided Paper Pad
- Birds & Blossoms double-sided Creative Scraps
- Cream felt
- White tissue paper
- Cupcake Party Large stamp set
- Dye ink pads: dark brown, light brown
- Light brown crackle paint
- Light brown Glimmer Mist
- Chipboard scroll
- 4 light green buttons in various sizes
- 9 green small self-adhesive gems
- 40 inches ¼-inch-wide peach silk ribbon
- 7½ inches 1⅜-inch-wide cream crochet lace decorative trim
- Nestabilities® die templates: Long Classic Scalloped Rectangles LG (#S4-143), Long Classic Rectangles LG (#S4-142), Standard Circles LG (#S4-114)
- Manual die-cutting and embossing machine
- Paintbrush
- Sewing machine with cream and green thread
- Glitter glue: iridescent, light green
- Adhesive foam dots
- Adhesive dots
- Paper adhesive

Tie each length into a bow. Layer and adhere to card front using adhesive dots. Attach tissue carnation over bows using an adhesive dot.

Thread all buttons with green thread; tie knots on backs. Trim ends. Using adhesive dots, attach buttons to card front as shown. Embellish card front with gems as desired.

Sources: Card stock from WorldWin Papers; Paper Pad, Birds & Blossoms Creative Scraps and stamp set from Crafty Secrets Publications; crackle paint and Stickles glitter glue from Ranger Industries Inc.; Glimmer Mist from Tattered Angels; chipboard scroll from Maya Road; ribbons from May Arts; die templates from Spellbinders™ Paper Arts.

Happy Birthday Tag

Ink front of one tag dark brown. Machine-stitch along edges. Adhere remaining tag to back of inked tag.

Using Long Classic Scalloped Rectangles LG die template, die-cut/emboss 1⅝ x 3¼-inch (#2), 2⅛ x 4¼ (#3) and 2⅝ x 5¼-inch (#4) scalloped rectangles from three different printed papers. Machine-stitch outer edges of all scalloped rectangles. Referring to photo and using foam dots, attach scalloped rectangles to tag as shown.

Wrap lace trim around bottom of tag; secure ends to back.

Cut a 3 x ¾-inch strip from cream striped paper; V-notch right end; ink edges light brown. Using dark brown ink, stamp "Happy Birthday" onto strip. Adhere left edge of strip to tag front as shown, allowing right end of strip to hang off edge of tag.

Paint chipboard scroll with crackle paint; let dry. Embellish with light green glitter glue; let dry. Adhere to tag as shown.

Die-cut/emboss Birds & Blossoms image with 2⅛ x 4¼-inch (#3) Mega Ovals LG die template. Die-cut/emboss a scalloped oval from floral printed paper using 1⅞ x 4-inch (#3) Mega Classic Scalloped Ovals LG die template. Adhere ovals together using foam dots. Referring to photo, attach layered ovals to tag with foam dots.

Tie a bow with multiple loops with peach ribbon. Set aside.

Following Tissue-Paper Carnations instructions on page 7, form a flower out of white tissue paper; spray with Glimmer Mist; let dry. Apply light brown ink and iridescent glitter glue to edges of flower. Layer and adhere peach bow and flower to tag front as shown.

String buttons with cream or green thread; tie knots on backs and trim ends. Attach to tag as desired using adhesive dots.

Punch a hole through scalloped rectangle covering tag's hole. Fold yellow ribbon in half and thread through hole as shown. Knot each end of ribbon.

Sources: Card stock from WorldWin Papers; Paper Pad, Birds & Blossoms Creative Scraps and stamp set from Crafty Secrets Publications; crackle paint and Stickles glitter glue from Ranger Industries Inc.; Glimmer Mist from Tattered Angels; chipboard scroll from Maya Road; ribbon from May Arts; die templates from Spellbinders™ Paper Arts.

Happy Birthday Candy Wrapper

Carefully remove outer wrapper of candy bar. Using wrapper as a template, cut a new wrapper from brown card stock. Wrap card-stock wrapper around candy bar; secure ends to back.

Cut a 6 x 9-inch piece from cream printed paper; machine-stitch outer edges. Wrap piece around candy bar. Secure ends to back.

Materials

- 2 (3⅛ x 6¼-inch) cream tags
- Classic Double-Sided Paper Pad
- Birds & Blossoms double-sided Creative Scraps
- White tissue paper
- Cupcake Party Large stamp set
- Dye ink pads: dark brown, light brown
- Light brown crackle paint
- Light brown Glimmer Mist
- Chipboard scroll
- 6 light green buttons in various sizes
- ¼-inch-wide silk ribbon: 34 inches peach, 14 inches light yellow
- 5½ inches 1⅜-inch-wide cream crochet lace decorative trim
- Nestabilities die templates: Long Classic Scalloped Rectangles LG (#S4-143), Mega Classic Scalloped Ovals LG (#S5-024), Mega Ovals LG (#S5-023), Standard Circles LG (#S4-114)
- Manual die-cutting and embossing machine
- Paintbrush
- ⅛-inch hole punch
- Sewing machine with cream and green thread
- Glitter glue: iridescent, light green
- Adhesive foam dots
- Adhesive dots
- Paper adhesive

Did You Know?

You can create flower embellishments with Nestabilities.

Happy Birthday
Happy Birthday
Happy Birthday

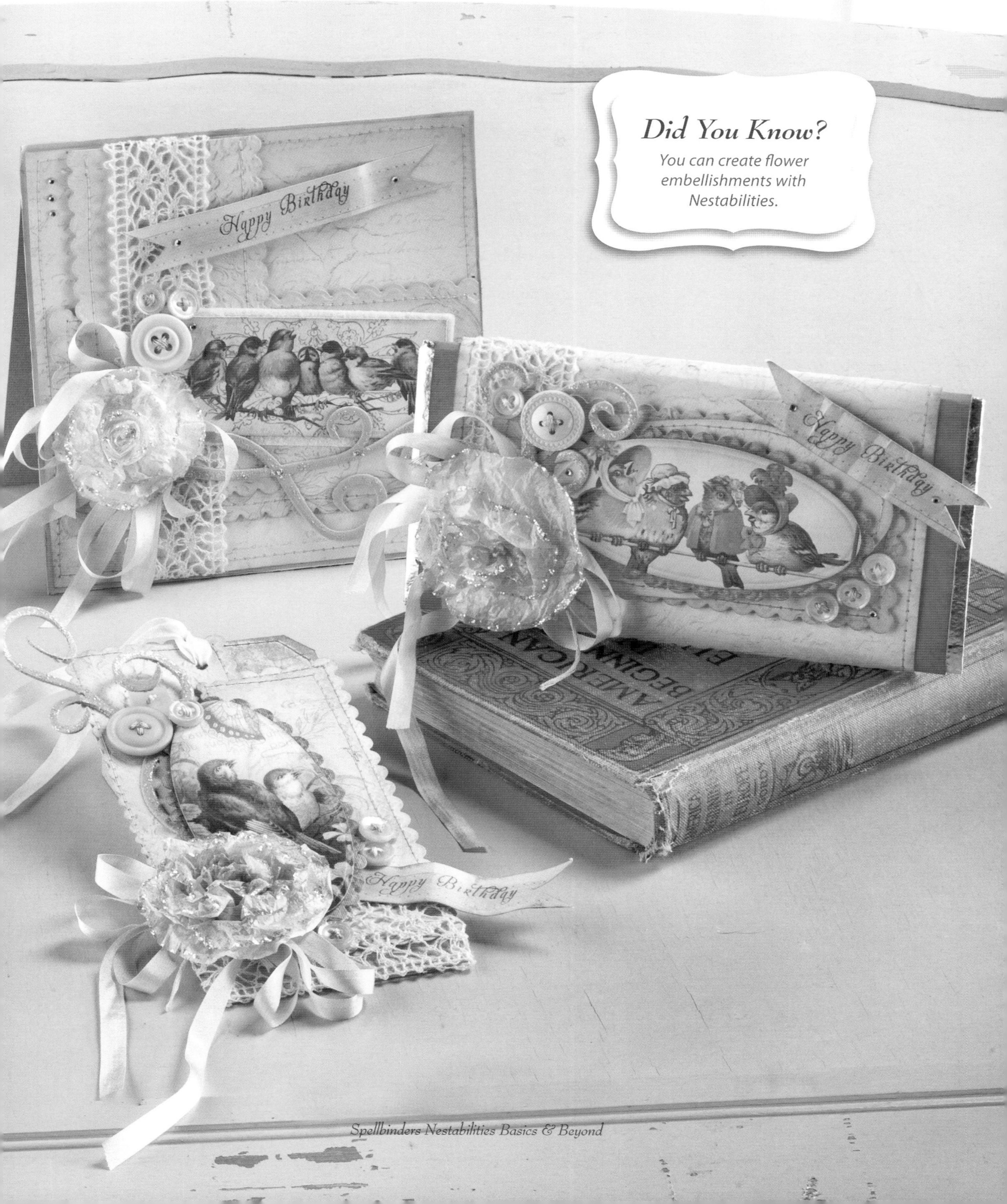

Wrap lace trim around left edge of printed-paper wrapper. Secure ends to back.

Using 5¼ x 2⅝-inch (#4) Long Classic Scalloped Rectangles LG die template, die-cut/emboss a scalloped rectangle from dark cream printed paper. Machine-stitch outer edges. Using foam dots, attach centered to candy-bar front.

Using 5 x 2⅜-inch (#4) Mega Ovals LG die template, die-cut/emboss an oval from light green printed paper; machine-stitch around edge with cream thread. Using foam dots, attach to scalloped rectangle as shown.

Using a 4 x 1⅞-inch (#3) Mega Ovals LG die template, die-cut/emboss an oval from Birds & Blossoms images; set aside.

Die-cut a scalloped oval from floral printed paper using 4¼ x 2⅛-inch (#3) Mega Classic Scalloped Ovals LG die template. Attach Birds & Blossoms oval to scalloped oval using foam dots. Attach layered ovals to candy-bar front as shown, using foam dots.

Paint chipboard scroll with crackle paint; let dry. Embellish scroll with light green glitter glue; let dry. Adhere to upper left corner of scalloped rectangle.

Thread all buttons with green or cream thread; tie knots on backs and trim ends. Using adhesive dots, attach buttons to candy-bar front as desired.

Cut peach ribbon into two equal lengths. Tie a bow with each length. Layer bows together; wrap a 5-inch piece of green thread around middle of bows; tie knot. Trim ends of thread.

Following Tissue-Paper Carnations instructions on page 7, form a flower out of white tissue paper; spray with Glimmer Mist; let dry. Apply light brown ink and iridescent glitter glue to edges of flower. Layer and adhere peach bow and flower to candy-bar front as shown.

Cut a 3½ x ¾-inch strip from cream striped paper; V-notch both ends. Using dark brown ink, stamp "Happy Birthday" onto strip. Crinkle strip and attach to upper right corner of candy wrapper using two layers of foam dots on each end.

Attach gems as desired. ■

Sources: *Card stock from WorldWin Papers; Paper Pad, Birds & Blossoms Creative Scraps and stamp set from Crafty Secrets Publications; crackle paint and Stickles glitter glue from Ranger Industries Inc.; Glimmer Mist from Tattered Angels; chipboard scroll from Maya Road; ribbons from May Arts; die templates from Spellbinders™ Paper Arts.*

Materials

- Large candy bar
- Brown card stock
- Classic Double-Sided Paper Pad
- Birds & Blossoms double-sided Creative Scraps
- White tissue paper
- Cupcake Party Large stamp set
- Dye ink pads: dark brown, light brown
- Light brown crackle paint
- Light brown Glimmer Mist
- Chipboard scroll
- 5 light green buttons in various sizes
- 4 green small self-adhesive gems
- 36 inches ¼-inch-wide peach silk ribbon
- 8 inches 1⅜-inch-wide cream crochet lace decorative trim
- Nestabilities die templates: Long Classic Scalloped Rectangles LG (#S4-143), Mega Classic Scalloped Ovals LG (#S5-024), Mega Ovals LG (#S5-023), Standard Circles LG (#S4-114)
- Manual die-cutting and embossing machine
- Paintbrush
- Sewing machine with cream and green thread
- Glitter glue: iridescent, light green
- Adhesive foam dots
- Adhesive dots
- Paper adhesive

Sweet Surprises

DESIGNS BY **MARY SNYDER**

Materials

- Printed papers:
  Vintage Drawing Paper,
  So Sophie Brothers &
  Sisters Petite Blue Floral,
  Road Show Text Tiles
- Hot pink tissue paper
- Sweet Kids stamp set
- Green ink pad
- Colored pencils
- Clear large glitter
- 3½ inches ⅜-inch-wide
  green gingham ribbon
- Nestabilities® die
  templates: Standard
  Circles SM (#S4-116),
  Petite Scalloped Circles
  SM (#S4-117), Petite
  Scalloped Circles LG
  (#S4-115)
- Manual die-cutting and
  embossing machine
- Silver glitter glue
- Double-sided tape
- Paper adhesive

Beautiful Dreamer Card

Form a 4 x 4-inch top-folded card from Vintage Drawing Paper. Following Making a Shaped Card instructions on page 5, die-cut/emboss card with 3½-inch (#5) Petite Scalloped Circles LG die template.

In the same manner, die-cut/emboss two 3½-inch (#5) scalloped circles from Text Tiles paper. Adhere a Text Tiles scalloped circle to front and back of card.

Using 3¼-inch (#5) Petite Scalloped Circles SM die template, die-cut/emboss a scalloped circle from Brothers & Sisters Petite Blue Floral paper. Adhere to card front.

Stamp child in hammock onto Vintage Drawing Paper; color with pencils and apply glitter glue to hearts. Let dry. Following Die Cutting Stamped Images instructions on page 4, and using Standard Circles SM 3-inch (#6) die template, die-cut stamped area. Adhere to card front.

Tie a knot 1 inch from one end of ribbon; trim opposite end to 1 inch. Adhere to card front as shown.

Using 1½-inch (#1) Petite Scalloped Circles SM die template and following Tissue-Paper Carnations instructions on page 7, die-cut hot pink tissue paper and form a carnation. Decorate carnation by applying paper adhesive and glitter. Attach to card front using double-sided tape.

Sources: *Vintage Drawing Paper printed paper from Jenni Bowlin Studio; So Sophie Brothers & Sisters Petite Blue Floral printed paper from My Mind's Eye; Road Show Text Tiles printed paper from Fancy Pants Designs; stamp set from Crafty Secrets Publications; die templates from Spellbinders™ Paper Arts; Stickles glitter glue from Ranger Industries Inc.*

My Friend Gift Box

Cut enough kraft paper to cover gift box. Paint kraft paper with watered-down acrylic paint; paint back and forth in straight lines leaving stroke marks for texture. Let dry completely.

Stamp images onto painted paper; color hearts with marker. Detail hearts with glitter glue. Let dry.

Wrap gift box with stamped/painted paper. Wrap ribbon around box as shown and secure ends with paper adhesive. Wrap raffia around box and tie a bow at top. Trim ends as desired. Attach lengths of curled pink ribbon to either side of bow as desired.

Following Tissue-Paper Carnations instructions on page 7, and using various sizes of Classic Scalloped Circles LG and Petite Scalloped Circles SM die templates, form six small carnations and one large carnation from hot pink and kraft-color tissue paper. Embellish carnations using adhesive and glitter. Attach carnations to top of gift box with double-sided tape.

Stamp multiple hearts and "my friend" onto Vintage Drawing Paper. Following Die Cutting Stamped Images instructions page 4, die-cut various-sized hearts from stamped areas using Classic Heart die templates. Repeat all heart die cuts with unstamped Vintage Drawing Paper.

Using Classic Scalloped Heart die templates, die-cut hearts from hot pink tissue paper slightly larger than stamped hearts. Adhere stamped and unstamped paper hearts to either side of tissue-paper hearts, sandwiching ends of raffia on gift box between hearts as desired. Attach remaining hearts to box using double-sided tape.

Sources: *Printed paper from Jenni Bowlin Studio; stamp set from Crafty Secrets Publications; die templates from Spellbinders™ Paper Arts; Stickles glitter glue from Ranger Industries Inc.*

Materials

- Gift box
- Kraft paper
- Vintage Drawing Paper printed paper
- Tissue paper: hot pink, kraft
- Sweet Kids stamp set
- Green ink pad
- White acrylic paint
- Hot pink marker
- Clear large glitter
- 3/8-inch-wide green gingham ribbon
- Natural raffia
- Pink curling ribbon
- Nestabilities die templates: Classic Scalloped Heart (#S4-137), Classic Heart (#S4-136), Petite Scalloped Circles SM (#S4-117), Classic Scalloped Circles LG (#S4-124)
- Manual die-cutting and embossing machine
- Paintbrush
- Silver glitter glue
- Double-sided tape
- Paper adhesive

Did You Know?

When you combine SM and LG Nestabilities they graduate in size in 1/8-inch increments.

Did You Know?

Spellbinders die templates help you to create apertures (window openings) in cards, bags, layouts and more.

Thanks Gift Bag

Using 2¾-inch (#5) Standard Circles LG die template, die-cut a circle window from front of gift bag following Making Windows instructions on page 5.

Using 3¼-inch (#5) Petite Scalloped Circles SM die template, die-cut a scalloped circle from clear page protector; set aside.

Following Making Frames instructions on page 6 and using 3¼-inch (#5) Petite Scalloped Circles SM and 2⅝-inch (#5) Standard Circles SM die templates, create a frame from Brothers & Sisters Petite Blue Floral paper.

Run frame through sticker machine. Adhere over clear scalloped circle. Attach to gift bag over die-cut window.

Stamp "Thanks" onto Vintage Drawing Paper. Using 1¼ x 1⅜-inch (#2) Classic Heart die template and following Die Cutting Stamped Images instructions on page 4, die-cut stamped area. Die-cut another heart from unstamped Vintage Drawing Paper.

Using 1½ x 1⅝-inch (#2) Classic Scalloped Heart die template, die-cut two hearts from hot pink tissue paper. Die-cut three 1 x 1⅛-inch (#1) scalloped hearts from hot pink tissue paper. Adhere hearts to gift bag as shown.

Using 1½-inch (#1) Petite Scalloped Circles SM die template and following Tissue-Paper Carnations instructions on page 7, die-cut hot pink tissue paper and form a carnation. Decorate carnation by applying paper adhesive and glitter.

Cut a piece of gingham ribbon; tie knot and trim ends. Using double-sided tape, layer and attach ribbon and carnation to gift bag.

Fold down top of bag. Punch two holes through folded section of bag. Thread a length of curling ribbon through holes; tie a bow; curl ends. Tie a small piece of gingham ribbon around center of bow; tie knot; trim ends.

Decorate candy as desired and place inside gift bag. ■

Sources: *Vintage Drawing Paper printed papers from Jenni Bowlin Studio; So Sophie Brothers & Sisters Petite Blue Floral printed paper from My Mind's Eye; stamp set from Crafty Secrets Publications; die templates from Spellbinders™ Paper Arts.*

Materials

- White gift bag
- Printed papers: Vintage Drawing Paper, So Sophie Brothers & Sisters Petite Blue Floral
- Hot pink tissue paper
- Clear page protector
- Sweet Kids stamp set
- Green ink pad
- Clear large glitter
- ⅜-inch-wide green/white gingham ribbon
- Pink curling ribbon
- Candy
- Nestabilities die templates: Classic Scalloped Heart (#S4-137), Classic Heart (#S4-136), Petite Scalloped Circles SM (#S4-117), Standard Circles SM (#S4-116), Standard Circles LG (#S4-114)
- Manual die-cutting and embossing machine
- Sticker machine
- ⅛-inch hole punch
- Double-sided tape
- Paper adhesive

A Very Merry Christmas

DESIGNS BY **ASHLEY CANNON NEWELL**

A Merry Christmas to You Card

Form a 4¼ x 5½-inch top-folded card from olive green card stock.

Stamp a 4 x 5¼-inch piece of kraft card stock with pattern stamp. Wrap red ribbon around kraft panel as shown; secure ends to back.

Using craft knife, cut two vertical slots large enough for seam binding to fit through 2⅜ inches above bottom edge of kraft panel and 1 inch from each side. Cut seam binding into two equal lengths. Thread a length of seam binding through a cut slot; tie in bow. Repeat to tie second length of seam binding onto other side of kraft panel. Adhere panel to card front.

Die-cut/emboss a 3⅛-inch (#4) star from olive green card stock using Stars Five die template. Attach to center of card front using foam dots.

Stamp "Merry Christmas" image onto kraft card stock. Following Die Cutting Stamped Images instructions on page 4, die-cut image with 2⅜-inch (#4) Standard Circles LG die template. Die-cut/emboss a 2⅜-inch circle from red card stock. Trim around stamped image as shown. Adhere stamped circle to red circle. Attach layered circle to olive green star using foam dots.

Attach gems as shown.

Sources: *Card stock and ribbon from Papertrey Ink; stamp set from Waltzingmouse Stamps; ink pad from Ranger Industries Inc.; self-adhesive gems from Kaisercraft; die templates from Spellbinders™ Paper Arts.*

Materials

- Card stock: kraft, olive green, red
- Very Vintage Christmas stamp set
- Olive green dye ink pad
- 7 inches ⅝-inch-wide red grosgrain ribbon
- 25 inches ½-inch-wide olive green seam binding
- 2 red small self-adhesive gems
- Nestabilities® die templates: Stars Five (#S4-092), Standard Circles LG (#S4-114)
- Manual die-cutting and embossing machine
- Craft knife
- Adhesive foam dots
- Instant-dry paper glue

Did You Know?

There are companies that make stamps to match Spellbinders Nestabilities and Shapeabilties die templates.

A Merry Christmas to You Gift Box

Stamp a 7½ x 8-inch piece of kraft card stock with pattern stamp. Referring to Box Lid diagram, score and fold along dashed lines and cut along solid lines. Adhere corners together to form lid. In the same manner, create box base from a 8¼ x 7¾-inch piece of kraft card stock referring to Box Base diagram.

Adhere ribbon across box lid as shown; secure ends to inside edges of box.

Die-cut/emboss a 3⅛-inch (#4) star using Stars Five die template and olive green card stock. Attach to center of box lid using foam dots.

Stamp "Merry Christmas" image onto kraft card stock. Following the Die Cutting Stamped Images instructions on page 4, die-cut image with 2⅜-inch (#4) Standard Circles LG die template. Die-cut/emboss a 2⅜-inch circle from red card stock.

Trim around stamped image as shown. Adhere stamped circle to red circle. Attach circle to olive green star using foam dots.

Sources: *Card stock and ribbon from Papertrey Ink; stamp set from Waltzingmouse Stamps; ink pad from Ranger Industries Inc.; die templates from Spellbinders™ Paper Arts.*

Materials

- Card stock: kraft, olive green, red
- Very Vintage Christmas stamp set
- Olive green dye ink pad
- 10¾ inches ⅝-inch-wide red grosgrain ribbon
- Nestabilities die templates: Stars Five (#S4-092), Standard Circles LG (#S-114)
- Manual die-cutting and embossing machine
- Scoring tool
- Adhesive foam dots
- Instant-dry paper glue

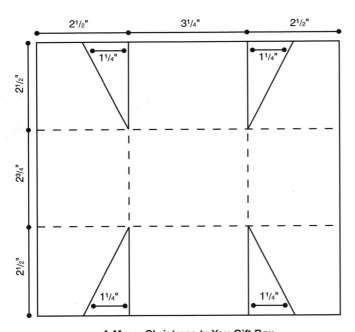

A Merry Christmas to You Gift Box
Box Base
Cut on solid lines; fold and score dashed lines

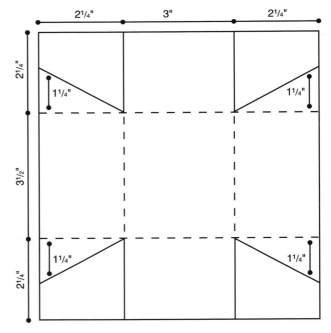

A Merry Christmas to You Gift Box
Box Lid
Cut on solid lines; score and fold on dashed lines

Spellbinders Nestabilities Basics & Beyond

Christmas Wishes Sachets & Tag

Using 3⅞-inch (#5) Stars Five die template, die-cut four stars from both olive green and red fabric, for a total of eight stars.

To form four star sachets, pair up eight die-cut fabric stars. Adhere all but one edge of paired stars together with craft glue; let dry completely. Fill stars with potpourri, adhere remaining edges closed. Let dry completely.

Using needle and thread, sew a button to center of each sachet.

Using white ink, stamp "Christmas Wishes" onto red card stock. Following Die Cutting Stamped Images instructions on page 4, die-cut around stamped area using 2⅜ x 3-inch (#4) Large Labels die template.

Using olive green ink, stamp a decorative frame onto kraft card stock. Following Making Frames instructions on page 6, die-cut a frame from stamped area using 2⅜ x 3-inch (#4) Large Labels die template and 1¾ x 2¼-inch (#3) Classic Ovals LG die template. Attach frame over stamped label using foam dots; trim foam dots down when needed. Punch hole and attach eyelet centered to top edge of tag.

Using olive green ink, stamp two holly leaves onto kraft card stock. Cut out leaves; attach to tag front as shown using foam dots. Attach red jewels to holly and stamped image as desired. ■

Sources: Card stock, ribbon and buttons from Papertrey Ink; fabrics from Michael Miller Fabrics; stamp set from Waltzingmouse Stamps; self-adhesive gems from Kaisercraft; die templates from Spellbinders™ Paper Arts.

Materials

- Card stock: kraft, red
- Printed fabric: red, olive green
- Very Vintage Christmas stamp set
- Ink pads: olive green dye, white craft
- 7 inches ⅝-inch-wide red grosgrain ribbon
- Red metallic string
- 6 red small self-adhesive gems
- Buttons: 2 red, 2 olive green
- Antique silver ¼-inch eyelet
- Dry potpourri
- Nestabilities die templates: Large Labels (#S4-168), Classic Ovals LG (#S4-110), Stars Five (#S4-092)
- Manual die-cutting and embossing machine
- ³⁄₁₆-inch hole punch
- Eyelet-setting tool
- Sewing needle and white thread
- Adhesive foam dots
- Liquid craft glue
- Instant-dry paper glue

Spirit of Christmas

DESIGNS BY **BECCA FEEKEN**

Spirit of Christmas Card

Form a 5½ x 7½-inch top-folded card from white card stock.

Adhere a 5⅛ x 7⅛-inch piece of white card stock to red card stock; trim a small border.

Using 3¾ x 5¾ (#6) Curved Rectangles die template, die-cut/emboss a curved rectangle from both white and red card stock. With short edge of red curved rectangle horizontal,

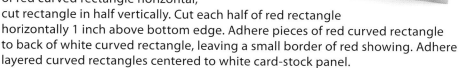

cut rectangle in half vertically. Cut each half of red rectangle horizontally 1 inch above bottom edge. Adhere pieces of red curved rectangle to back of white curved rectangle, leaving a small border of red showing. Adhere layered curved rectangles centered to white card-stock panel.

Using 2⅞ x 6-inch (#5) Long Classic Rectangles LG die template, die-cut/emboss a rectangle from red card stock. Using 2⅝ x 5½-inch (#5) Long Classic Rectangles SM die template, die-cut/emboss a rectangle from white card stock. Layer and adhere rectangles centered to top of curved rectangle.

Stamp sentiment onto white card stock. Sprinkle with clear embossing powder; heat-emboss using embossing heat tool. Following Die Cutting Stamped Images instructions on page 4, die-cut/emboss sentiment using 2½ x 3⅝-inch (#4) Petite Ovals LG die template.

Using 2¾ x 3⅞-inch (#5) Petite Ovals SM die template, die-cut/emboss an oval from red card stock. Attach sentiment to red oval using foam tape.

Using 3 x 4-inch (#5) Petite Scalloped Ovals SM die template, die-cut/emboss a scalloped oval from white card stock. Attach scalloped oval to back of layered oval using foam tape. In the same manner, attach oval to top of layered rectangle on card front.

Die-cut bottom edge of a 5⅛ x 2⅜-inch piece of white card stock using Lotus Petite die template. Attach ⅛ inch above bottom edge of white panel with foam tape.

Wrap ribbon around panel as shown; tie bow; V-notch ends. Secure bow with adhesive. Using foam tape, attach panel to card front.

Die-cut/emboss three round snowflakes and five star snowflakes from white card stock using Snowflake Wonder die templates. Using foam tape, layer three star snowflakes over round snowflakes. Attach remaining star snowflakes and layered snowflakes over Lotus border as shown. Embellish snowflakes with red pearls.

Attach white pearls to card front as shown.

Sources: *Stamp from Quietfire Design; ribbon and flat-back pearls from Michaels Stores Inc.; die templates from Spellbinders™ Paper Arts.*

Materials

- Card stock:
  white 120 lb, red
- Hold on to the Spirit of
  Christmas stamp
- Red pigment ink pad
- Clear embossing powder
- Flat-back pearls:
  5 red, 10 white
- 24 inches 1⅝-inch-wide
  red wire-edged ribbon
- Nestabilities® die
  templates: Curved
  Rectangles (#S5-006),
  Long Classic Rectangles
  LG (#S4-142), Long Classic
  Rectangles SM (#S4-144),
  Petite Ovals LG (#S4-138),
  Petite Ovals SM (#S4-
  140), Petite Scalloped
  Ovals SM (#S4-141)
- Lotus Borderabilities®
  Petite die templates
  (#S4-240)
- Snowflake Wonder
  Shapeabilities® die
  templates (#S4-085)
- Manual die-cutting and
  embossing machine
- Embossing heat tool
- Adhesive foam tape
- Paper adhesive

Naughty or Nice List

Create a notebook cover by cutting a strip of red card stock wide enough and long enough to cover entire notebook so that it will create an overlapping top and bottom flap on front of notebook. Score red card-stock strip where needed and adhere strip to notebook using double-sided tape.

Using black ink, stamp "Naughty Nice" onto bottom flap; sprinkle with embossing powder and heat-emboss using embossing heat tool.

Using red ink, stamp "Oh Santa" saying onto white card stock. Sprinkle with embossing powder; heat-emboss using embossing heat tool. Following Die Cutting Stamped Images instructions on page 4, die-cut/emboss an oval around sentiment using 2½ x 3⅝-inch (#4) Petite Ovals LG die template.

Die-cut/emboss an oval from red card stock using 2¾ x 3⅞-inch (#5) Petite Ovals SM die template. Attach sentiment oval to red oval using foam tape.

Using 3 x 4-inch (#5) Petite Scalloped Ovals SM die template, die-cut/emboss two scalloped ovals from white card stock.

Adhere one half of magnetic snap to back of one scalloped oval near bottom edge. Adhere top half of scalloped oval with magnetic snap to inside top flap of note-book cover. Attach remaining half of magnetic snap to inside bottom notebook cover flap, aligning magnets so cover will snap closed.

Adhere remaining scalloped oval to front of notebook cover, aligning scalloped edges of ovals. Using foam tape, attach sentiment oval centered to scalloped ovals.

Embellish cover with pearls as shown. Wrap ribbon around bottom flap. Tie bow; V-notch ends.

Sources: Stamps from Quietfire Design; ribbon and flat-back pearls from Michaels Stores Inc.; fine-detail ink pad from Tsukineko LLC; die templates from Spellbinders™ Paper Arts.

Materials

- Card stock:
  white 120 lb, red
- Very Vintage Christmas stamp set
- Red pigment ink pad
- Clear embossing powder
- 16 red flat-back pearls
- Red brad
- Red twine
- Nestabilities die templates: Petite Scalloped Circles LG (#S4-115), Standard Circles LG (#S4-114)
- Lotus Borderabilities Petite die templates (#S4-240)
- Shapeabilities die templates: Snowflake Wonder (#S4-085), Tags Five (#S4-081)
- Manual die-cutting and embossing machine
- Embossing heat tool
- Paper piercer
- Scoring tool
- Adhesive foam tape
- Paper adhesive

Materials

- Card stock:
  white 120 lb, red
- Small notebook
- Stamps: Naughty Nice, Oh Santa I've Been Good
- Ink pads: red pigment, black fine-detail
- Clear embossing powder
- Flat-back pearls: 4 white, 5 red small
- 1⅝-inch-wide red wire-edged ribbon
- Small magnetic snap
- Nestabilities die templates: Petite Ovals LG (#S4-138), Petite Ovals SM (#S4-140), Petite Scalloped Ovals SM (#S4-141)
- Manual die-cutting and embossing machine
- Scoring tool
- Embossing heat tool
- Double-sided tape
- Adhesive foam tape
- Paper adhesive

Gift Box

Using a 12 x 12-inch piece of white card stock, create a box lid referring to Box Lid diagram on page 40. Score and fold along dashed lines and cut along solid lines, adhere sides together to create box lid. Using a 11¼ x 11¼-inch piece white card stock create a box base referring to Box Base diagram on page 40. Score and fold along dashed lines and cut along solid lines, adhere sides together to create box base.

Adhere a 17 x 2-inch strip of red card stock around box lid as shown.

Using Lotus Petite die template, die-cut/emboss one long edge on four 4⅛ x 1⅝-inch strips of white card stock. Adhere a die-cut strip over red strip on each side of box lid.

Using Snowflake Wonder die template, die-cut/emboss 16 star snowflakes and eight round snowflakes from white card stock. Using foam tape, adhere a star snowflake over each round snowflake. Adhere snowflakes to die-cut strips around box lid as shown using foam tape. Embellish snowflakes with red pearls.

Using foam tape, attach a 4 x 4-inch square of red card stock to top of box lid.

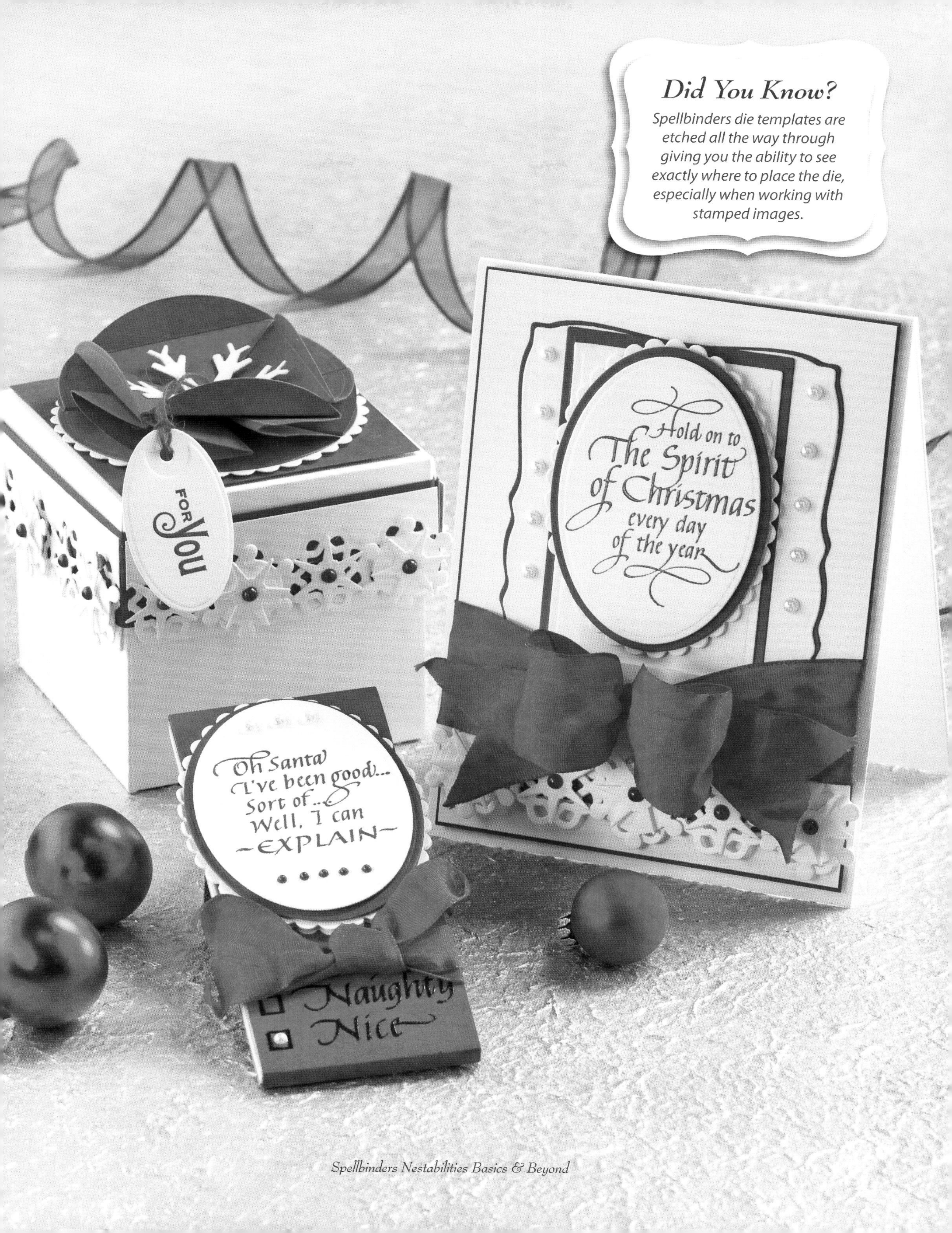

FOR YOU
Hold on to The Spirit of Christmas every day of the year
Oh Santa I've been good... Sort of... Well, I can ~EXPLAIN~
Naughty
Nice

Did You Know?

Spellbinders die templates are etched all the way through giving you the ability to see exactly where to place the die, especially when working with stamped images.

Following Spirit of Christmas Box-Top Technique instructions on page 7, create decorative box-top piece from red card stock. Adhere bottom edge of red pie shapes to white scalloped circle as shown.

Die-cut/emboss a large snowflake from white card stock using Snowflake Wonder die template. Place large snowflake centered on top of red pie-shape pieces. Pierce a hole through center of snowflake, through center of pie shapes and scalloped circle; insert brad. Attach to top of box using foam tape.

Stamp "For You" onto white card stock. Sprinkle with clear embossing powder; heat-emboss using embossing heat tool. Following Die Cutting Stamped Images instructions on page 4, die-cut/emboss sentiment using 2⅝ x 1⅝-inch (Oval) Tags Five die template. Thread red twine through hole on tag and around brad; tie knot; trim ends. ◼

Sources: *Stamp set from Waltzingmouse Stamps; flat-back pearls from Michaels Stores Inc.; die templates from Spellbinders™ Paper Arts.*

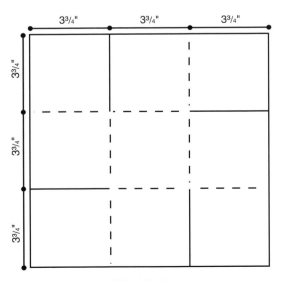

Spirit of Christmas
Box Base
Cut on solid lines; score and fold dashed lines

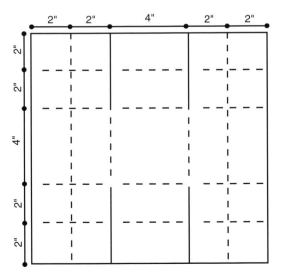

Spirit of Christmas
Box Lid
Cut on solid lines; score and fold dashed lines

Holiday Sparkle

DESIGNS BY **JULIE GAIL**

Happy Holidays Card

Project note: *Sentiment can also be created using rub-on transfers, stamps or by hand-printing.*

Form a 5½ x 6-inch side-folded card from lime green card stock.

Using Standard Circles LG die templates, die-cut a 1⅜-inch (#2) circle and a 1⅞-inch (#3) circle from red glitter card stock. Die-cut a 2⅜-inch (#4) circle from gold glitter card stock. Die-cut a photo of your choice using 1⅞-inch (#3) circle die template.

Following Making Frames instructions on page 6, die-cut a circle frame using 1⅞-inch (#3) and 1⅜-inch (#2) circle die templates and red glitter card stock.

Adhere red glitter frame over die-cut photo; adhere to gold glitter circle. Cut rickrack into two 1¾-inch lengths and one 1-inch length. Adhere lengths of rickrack to glitter circles as shown. Adhere glitter circles to card front as shown.

Cut two 5½ x ½-inch strips from green glitter card stock; adhere to top and bottom edges of card front. Use a computer to generate "Happy Holidays" onto light lime green card stock. Trim down to a 5½ x ¾-inch strip; adhere to card front as shown. Cut a 5½ x ⅛-inch strip from green glitter card stock; adhere to card front over ends of rickrack as shown.

Attach a gem to each side of sentiment. Tie three bows from gold metallic thread; adhere a bow to each glitter circle using adhesive dots.

Source: *Die templates from Spellbinders™ Paper Arts.*

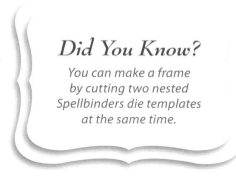

Did You Know?

You can make a frame by cutting two nested Spellbinders die templates at the same time.

Materials

- Card stock: lime green, light lime green
- Glitter card stock: green, red, gold
- Photo
- Gold metallic thread
- 4½ inches ⅛-inch-wide gold metallic rickrack
- 2 gold self-adhesive gems
- Standard Circles LG Nestabilities® die templates (#S4-114)
- Manual die-cutting and embossing machine
- Adhesive dots
- Paper adhesive
- Computer with printer

Photo Ornament

Option: Instead of using two photos for ornament center, use a computer to generate a holiday sentiment onto white card stock.

Following Making Frames instructions on page 6, create two scalloped frames using 4⅛-inch (#6) Classic Scalloped Circles LG die template, 1⅞-inch (#5) Standard Circles LG die template and red glitter card stock.

In the same manner, create two scalloped frames using 3⅜-inch (#5) Classic Scalloped Circles SM die template, 2⅜-inch (#4) Standard Circles LG die template and gold glitter card stock. Adhere a gold frame to each red frame.

Following Die Cutting Stamped Images instructions on page 4, die-cut two photos using ⅞-inch (#1) Standard Circles LG die template. Adhere a die-cut photo to each bottle cap.

Cut a 9-inch length of gold thread. Fold in half; slide three beads onto unfolded end of thread; knot unfolded ends together. Lay one bottle cap on work surface photo-side down. Place an adhesive dot onto back of bottle cap, lay knotted end of string onto adhesive dot. Attach remaining bottle cap photo-side up.

Adhere red frames together as shown, sandwiching gold thread between frames. *Note: The bottle caps and beads should be hanging inside the circle window.* Knot thread two times above frames forming a hanging loop.

Tie bow with gold ribbon; trim ends. Tie a small piece of gold thread around center of bow; trim ends. Adhere to front of ornament. Attach gems around gold frame on front of ornament, alternating colors as shown.

Source: Die templates from Spellbinders™ Paper Arts.

Materials

- White card stock (optional)
- Glitter card stock: red, gold
- 2 photos
- Gold metallic thread
- 7¾ inches ⅜-inch-wide gold metallic wire-edged ribbon
- 2 bottle caps
- Small beads: 1 gold, 2 green
- Self-adhesive gems: 11 gold, 11 silver
- Nestabilities die templates: Standard Circles LG (#S4-114), Classic Scalloped Circles LG (#S4-124), Classic Scalloped Circles SM (#S4-125)
- Manual die-cutting and embossing machine
- Adhesive dots
- Paper adhesive
- Computer with printer (optional)

Tabletop Tree

Glue one end of dowel into top of spool of thread.

Using Classic Scalloped Circles LG die templates, die-cut 2⅛-inch (#2), 3⅛-inch (#4) and 4⅛-inch (#6) scalloped circles from both green glitter card stock and scrap paper.

Following Making a Tree instructions on page 8, assemble tree.

Wrap gold wire around top of wooden dowel, leaving a 1½-inch length extending past end of dowel.

Die-cut two 1⅛-inch (#2) stars from gold glitter card stock using Stars Five die template. Adhere stars together over gold wire as shown, using an adhesive dot.

Attach gems to cones and star as shown. Tie a bow with ribbon; trim ends and attach to gold wire using a small piece of gold thread. Adhere bottom of wooden dowel into center of spool of thread. ■

Source: Die templates from Spellbinders™ Paper Arts.

Materials

- Glitter card stock: green, gold
- Scrap paper
- Gold metallic thread
- 4½-inch wooden dowel
- Light green drinking straw
- Green spool of thread
- 12 inches 18-gauge gold craft wire
- 6 inches ⅜-inch-wide metallic gold wire-edged ribbon
- Self-adhesive gems: 7 small light green, 8 medium dark green, 9 large light green
- Round brad
- Nestabilities die templates: Classic Scalloped Circles LG (#S4-124), Stars Five (#S4-092)
- Manual die-cutting and embossing machine
- Paper piercer
- Adhesive dots
- Paper adhesive

Happy Holidays

Mother's Day Tea

DESIGNS BY **TERRE FRY**

My Mom Card

Project notes: Ink edges of pieces brown as desired. If "My Mom" stamp cannot be found, use rub-on transfers, stickers or a computer to generate sentiment.

Form a 5 x 7-inch side-folded card from golden yellow card stock.

Cut a 4⅝ x 6⅝-inch rectangle from Domestic Goddess paper; machine-stitch along edges. Distress and ink edges brown. Adhere to card front.

Cut a 5 x 3-inch piece from Simple As A Pie paper; machine-stitch along edges. Distress and ink edges brown. Adhere to card front 1½ inches above bottom edge.

Using brown ink and following Reverse Stenciling instructions on page 6, die-cut/emboss a piece of Simple As A Pie paper using 2⅝ x 5¼-inch (#4) Long Classic Scalloped Rectangles LG die template. Using adhesive dots, attach to card front as shown.

In the same manner, reverse stencil and die-cut/emboss a 5 x 1¼-inch strip of Simple As A Pie Paper using Big Scalloped Border Grand die template. Distress short edges. Using foam squares, attach to card front ½ inch above bottom edge. Using adhesive dots, attach buttons to scalloped border.

Using 3½ x 4½-inch (#6) Petite Scalloped Ovals SM die template, die-cut/emboss a scalloped oval from rust card stock. Using 2¾ x 3⅞-inch (#5) Petite Ovals SM die template, die-cut/emboss desired image from Domestic Goddess paper. Attach oval to scalloped oval using foam squares. Adhere to card front as shown.

Stamp "My Mom" onto golden yellow card stock. Following Die Cutting Stamped Images and Reverse Stenciling instructions on pages 4 and 6, reverse stencil and die-cut sentiment using 1⅝-inch (#3) Standard Circles SM die template with brown ink.

Tie ribbon to one stickpin and lace to the other; trim ends. Tape stickpins to back of stamped circle. Using foam squares, attach circle to card front as shown.

Sources: *Card stock from Bazzill Basics Paper Inc. and WorldWin Papers; printed papers from Graphic 45; stickpins from Maya Road; die templates and Grand Calibur™ machine from Spellbinders™ Paper Arts.*

Materials

- Card stock: golden yellow, rust
- Domestic Goddess double-sided printed papers: Domestic Goddess, Simple As A Pie
- "My Mom" stamp
- Ink pads: brown chalk, black dye
- 2 pearl stickpins
- 3 large brown buttons
- 2 inches ⅛-inch-wide white grosgrain ribbon
- 2½ inches ⅜-inch-wide black lace
- Sewing machine with white thread
- Nestabilities® die templates: Long Classic Scalloped Rectangles LG (#S4-143), Petite Scalloped Ovals SM (#S4-141), Petite Ovals SM (#S4-140), Standard Circles SM (#S4-116)
- Big Scalloped Border Grand Borderabilities® die templates (#S7-018)
- Grand Calibur™ manual die-cutting and embossing machine
- Sandpaper
- Tape
- Adhesive dots
- Adhesive foam squares
- Paper adhesive

Mother's Day Tea Invitation

Cut a 2⅞ x 10-inch piece from golden yellow card stock. Following Selective Die Cutting instructions on page 5, die-cut/emboss both short ends of golden yellow piece using 3 x 4-inch (#5) Petite Scalloped Oval SM die template. Cut a 2¾ x 7¾-inch piece of Tea Time paper, center and adhere to what will be the inside of the golden yellow piece.

With printed paper side faceup on work surface and long edge horizontal, score vertical lines 2½ inches and 3 inches from one scalloped end. Repeat to score vertical lines on opposite end. Fold at scored lines to form invitation.

Using 3⅞ x 2¾-inch (#5) Petite Ovals SM die template, die-cut/emboss an oval from Miss Manners paper. Cut oval in half. Adhere half ovals to top and bottom flap of invitation as shown. Using black ink, stamp "do join us for a TEA PARTY" onto top flap. Using red ink, stamp a teacup onto bottom flap; stamp steam above teacup using black ink.

Thread button with ribbon; tie knot on front; trim ends. Using an adhesive dot, attach button to bottom edge of top flap.

Did You Know?

You can choose to only emboss with a Spellbinders die template.

Stamp "FOR YOU" tag onto white card stock using black ink; cut out. Punch a ⅛-inch hole through top of tag; thread a length of jute through hole and tie a knot. Trim one end of jute next to knot and leave one end long. Using adhesive dots, attach tag below button as shown. Run long tail of jute up right side of invitation and attach using an adhesive dot.

Using black ink, stamp "AFTERNOON TEA" image onto white card stock; cut out. Attach centered inside invitation using foam squares.

Cut a 1⅝ x 1⅝-inch square from Miss Manners paper. Cut in half diagonally, forming two triangles. Adhere triangles to inside flaps.

To create a closure, cut a small piece of hook-and-loop tape. Attach one side to outside bottom flap and one to inside top flap making sure pieces align.

Sources: Card stock from WorldWin Papers; printed papers from Graphic 45; stamp set from Waltzingmouse Stamps; die templates from Spellbinders™ Paper Arts.

Materials

- Card stock: golden yellow, white
- Domestic Goddess double-sided printed papers: Miss Manners, Tea Time
- Afternoon Tea stamp set
- Ink pads: brown chalk, black dye, red dye
- Large brown button
- 3 inches ⅛-inch-wide white grosgrain ribbon
- Natural jute
- Nestabilities die templates: Petite Scalloped Ovals SM (#S4-141), Petite Ovals SM (#S4-140)
- Manual die-cutting and embossing machine
- Scoring tool
- ⅛-inch hole punch
- Hook-and-loop tape
- Adhesive dots
- Adhesive foam squares
- Paper adhesive

Materials

- Golden yellow card stock
- Domestic Goddess double-sided printed paper
- Black letter rub-on transfers
- Brown chalk ink pad
- 2 pearl stickpins
- Large brown button
- 2 inches ⅛-inch-wide white grosgrain ribbon
- 2½ inches ⅜-inch-wide black lace
- Nestabilities die templates: Petite Scalloped Ovals SM (#S4-141), Petite Ovals SM (#S4-140)
- Manual die-cutting and embossing machine
- Tape
- Adhesive dots
- Adhesive foam squares
- Paper adhesive

Mother's Day Place Card

Form a 4½ x 3-inch top-folded card from golden yellow card stock. Following Making a Shaped Card instructions on page 5, die-cut/emboss card using 4 x 3-inch (#5) Petite Scalloped Ovals SM die template. Using 2⅞ x 1¾-inch (#3) Petite Ovals SM die template, die-cut/emboss an oval from printed paper. Apply rub-on transfer letters to spell desired name.

Wrap lace around a stickpin; tie knot. Wrap ribbon around remaining stickpin; tie knot. Attach stickpins to back of oval using tape. Attach oval to card front using foam squares. Using an adhesive dot, adhere button to bottom right edge of oval. ■

Sources: Card stock from WorldWin Papers; printed paper from Graphic 45; rub-on transfers from Fiskars; stickpins from Maya Road; die templates from Spellbinders™ Paper Arts.

Remember When

DESIGNS BY **JUDY HAYES**

Best Wishes Card

Form a 6½ x 4½-inch top-folded card from cream card stock. Adhere a 6½ x 4½-inch piece of gold pearlescent card stock to card front; round all four corners of card.

Using 5¾ x 4-inch (#6) Curved Rectangles die template, die-cut/emboss a curved rectangle from ivory pearlescent card stock. Center and adhere to card front.

Emboss a 6 x 4½-inch piece of ivory pearlescent card stock using Fleur de Lis Pattern embossing template. Following Making Frames instructions on page 6 and using 5¼ x 3½-inch (#5) Curved Rectangles and 4⅜ x 2¾-inch (#6) Labels Four die templates, die-cut/emboss a frame from embossed ivory card stock.

Using window screen in the same manner as an embossing template, emboss a 4½ x 3¼-inch piece of cream card stock. Adhere ivory pearlescent frame on top of embossed piece of cream card stock. Wrap sheer ribbon around frame; tie bow on left side; trim ends. Center and adhere layered frame to card front.

In the same manner as before, emboss a 4 x 3-inch piece of ivory pearlescent card stock, using window screen as embossing template. Create a frame from embossed ivory pearlescent card stock in the same manner as before, using 3⅛ x 2⅛-inch (#3) Petite Ovals LG and 2¼ x 1⅜-inch (#2) Petite Ovals SM die templates.

Create another frame from gold pearlescent card stock using 3⅜ x 2¼-inch (#4) Petite Ovals SM and 2¼ x 1⅛-inch (#1) Petite Ovals LG die templates.

Using watermark ink, stamp "Best Wishes" onto cream card stock. Sprinkle with embossing powder; heat-emboss using embossing heat tool. Following Die Cutting Stamped Images instructions on page 4, die-cut sentiment using 3⅛ x 2⅛-inch (#3) Petite Ovals SM die template. Ink edges light brown. Layer and adhere frames and sentiment oval as shown. Using foam squares, attach sentiment to card front.

Tie a bow with striped ribbon; trim ends. Adhere below bow on card front using adhesive dots. Embellish card front with pearls as desired.

Sources: *Stamp set from JustRite; watermark ink pad from Tsukineko LLC; flat-back pearls from A Muse Art Stamps; die templates and embossing template from Spellbinders™ Paper Arts.*

Materials

- Pearlescent card stock: ivory, gold
- Cream card stock
- Thin chipboard sheets
- Victorian Nested Frames stamp set
- Ink pads: watermark, light brown dye
- Gold embossing powder
- Light pink small flat-back pearls
- Gold ribbon: 17½ inches 1-inch-wide sheer, 10 inches ⅝-inch-wide sheer striped
- Nestabilities® die templates: Labels Four (#S4-190), Curved Rectangles (#S5-006), Petite Ovals LG (#S4-138), Petite Ovals SM (#S4-140)
- Fleur de Lis Pattern Impressabilities™ embossing template (#I2-1014)
- Small piece of window screen
- Manual die-cutting and embossing machine
- ½-inch corner rounder
- Embossing heat tool
- Adhesive dots
- Adhesive foam squares
- Paper adhesive

Thank You Card

Form a 5½ x 3⅞-inch top-folded card from cream card stock; round corners.

Using 5¼ x 3½-inch (#5) Curved Rectangles die template, die-cut/emboss a curved rectangle from ivory pearlescent card stock. Center and adhere to card front.

Using window screen in the same manner as an embossing template, emboss a 5½ x 3¾-inch piece of gold pearlescent card stock. Die-cut embossed gold pearlescent card stock using 4½ x 3-inch (#4) Curved Rectangles die template. Center and adhere to card front.

Emboss a 5 x 3½-inch piece of ivory pearlescent card stock using Fleur de Lis Pattern embossing template. Following Making Frames instructions on page 6, create a frame with embossed ivory pearlescent card stock using 4⅜ x 2¾-inch (#6) Labels Four and 2⅝ x 1⅝-inch (#2) Petite Ovals LG die templates. Attach frame to card front as shown using foam squares.

Using watermark ink, stamp "Thank You" onto cream card stock. Sprinkle with embossing powder; heat-emboss using embossing heat tool. Following Die Cutting Stamped Images instructions on page 4, die-cut sentiment using 2¼ x 1⅛-inch (#1) Petite Ovals LG die template. Ink edges light brown. Attach to card front as shown using foam squares.

Sources: Stamp set from JustRite; watermark ink pad from Tsukineko LLC; die templates and embossing template from Spellbinders™ Paper Arts.

Materials

- Pearlescent card stock: ivory, gold
- Cream card stock
- Thin chipboard sheets
- Baroque Nested Frames stamp set
- Ink pads: watermark, light brown dye
- Gold embossing powder
- Nestabilities die templates: Labels Four (#S4-190), Curved Rectangles (#S5-006), Petite Ovals LG (#S4-138)
- Fleur de Lis Pattern Impressabilities embossing template (#I2-1014)
- Small piece of window screen
- Manual die-cutting and embossing machine
- ½-inch corner rounder
- Embossing heat tool
- Adhesive foam squares
- Paper adhesive

Remember When Memory Book

For front and back covers, cut two 8½ x 5½-inch rectangles each from chipboard, cream card stock and ivory pearlescent card stock. Using spray adhesive, adhere a cream rectangle to back of each chipboard rectangle. In the same manner, adhere an ivory pearlescent rectangle to front of each chipboard rectangle. Round four corners of both layered rectangles. Set one cover aside; this will be the back cover.

For front cover, following Making Frames instructions on page 6, die-cut/emboss a frame from ivory pearlescent card stock using 5¼ x 3½-inch (#5) and 5⅞ x 4-inch (#6) Curved Rectangles die templates.

Using window screen in the same manner as an embossing template, emboss a 6½ x 5-inch piece of cream card stock. Die-cut embossed piece using 5⅞ x 4-inch (#6) Curved Rectangle die template. Adhere ivory frame over cream curved rectangle. Adhere centered to front cover. Wrap sheer ribbon around album cover as shown; tie bow on left side; trim ends.

Using 4⅛ x 3⅝-inch (#6) Labels Five die template, die-cut/emboss a label from gold pearlescent card stock. Attach to album front as shown using foam squares.

Emboss a piece of ivory pearlescent card stock using Fleur de Lis Pattern embossing template. Create another frame from embossed ivory piece, in the same manner as before, using 4⅜ x 2¾-inch (#6) Labels Four and 3⅛ x 2⅛-inch Petite Ovals LG die templates.

Stamp sentiment onto cream card stock using watermark ink. Sprinkle sentiment with embossing powder; heat-emboss using embossing heat tool. Trim sentiment panel to fit behind embossed frame. Adhere embossed frame over sentiment panel. Adhere to front cover as shown.

Cut striped ribbon into two 10-inch lengths. Tie a bow with each length; trim ends. Using adhesive dots, attach a bow above and below bow on front cover. Embellish with small pearls as desired.

For album photo pages, cut several 8½ x 5½-inch rectangles from ivory pearlescent card stock; cut the same amount from cream card stock. Round all four corners on each piece. Adhere cream card-stock pieces to backs of ivory pearlescent pieces; this will provide support for photos and frames. In the same manner as for front cover, create frames for photos. Insert photos and desired notes inside frames; adhere frames to pages as desired.

Did You Know?

You can create shaped borders with the Grand Nestabilities.

Materials

- Pearlescent card stock: ivory, gold
- Cream card stock
- Thin chipboard sheets
- Cherish the Memories Nested Sentiments & Verse stamp set
- Ink pads: watermark, light brown dye
- Gold embossing powder
- Tan marker
- Light pink small flat-back pearls
- Gold ribbon: 31 inches 1-inch-wide sheer, 20 inches ⅝-inch-wide sheer striped
- 2 small silver book rings
- Nestabilities die templates: Labels Four (#S4-190), Curved Rectangles (#S5-006), Labels Five (#S4-229), Petite Ovals LG (#S4-138)
- Fleur de Lis Pattern Impressabilities embossing template (#I2-1014)
- Small piece of window screen
- Manual die-cutting and embossing machine
- Punches: ³⁄₁₆-inch hole, ½-inch corner rounder
- Marker airbrush system
- Embossing heat tool
- Water-based spray sealer
- Spray adhesive
- Adhesive dots
- Adhesive foam squares
- Paper adhesive

For album journaling pages, cut several 8½ x 5½-inch rectangles from cream card stock; round all four corners on each piece. Using watermark ink, stamp desired headings at center top of journaling pages such as "Family" and "Friends"; sprinkle headings with embossing powder and heat-emboss using embossing heat tool.

Use marker and airbrush system to apply color to silver book rings. Let dry completely. Spray with water-based spray sealer; dry completely.

Punch two ³⁄₁₆-inch holes through left side of each album page, and front and back covers; holes should be approximately 3¾ inches apart and ½ inch from left edge. Stack covers and album pages on top of each other. Slide book rings through holes and snap closed. ■

Sources: *Stamp set from JustRite; watermark ink pad from Tsukineko LLC; flat-back pearls from A Muse Art Stamps: Copic marker and Copic Airbrush System from Imagination International Inc.; die templates and embossing template from Spellbinders™ Paper Arts.*

Anniversary Ensemble

DESIGNS BY **KAZAN CLARK**

You're Invited Card

Form a 5 x 5-inch top-folded card from black card stock. Adhere a 4½ x 4½-inch piece of printed paper to lime green card stock; trim a small border. Wrap a 7-inch length of ribbon vertically around panel; secure ends to back. Adhere panel to card front as shown.

Hand-print, or use computer to generate, "You're Invited" onto white card stock. Following Die Cutting Stamped Images instructions on page 4, die-cut sentiment using 3¾ x 3¾-inch (#6) Labels Sixteen die template.

Following Making Frames instructions on page 6, create a frame from black card stock using 3¾ x 3¾-inch (#6) and 3⅛ x 3⅛-inch (#5) Labels Sixteen die templates. Adhere black frame over sentiment label. Adhere to card front as shown.

Using 1⅝ x 1⅝-inch (#2) and 1 x 1-inch (#1) Blossom Two die templates, die-cut/emboss two flowers from white card stock. Score lines across flower petals to form dimensional petals. Chalk edges of both flowers light brown. Layer and attach flowers to lower right corner of card front using adhesive dots.

Thread button using cream string, tie knot on back. Using adhesive dot, attach to center of flower.

Tie a bow with remaining length of ribbon; trim ends. Using adhesive dots, attach to card front above sentiment label.

Sources: *Card stock from WorldWin Papers; printed paper from 7gypsies; die templates from Spellbinders™ Paper Arts.*

Materials

- Card stock: black, lime green, white
- Avignon Decoration printed paper
- Light brown chalk
- 16 inches ¹¹⁄₁₆-inch-wide black/white striped satin ribbon
- Cream string
- White small button
- Black fine-tip marker
- Nestabilities® die templates: Blossom Two (#S4-232), Labels Sixteen (#S4-301)
- Manual die-cutting and embossing machine
- Scoring tool
- Adhesive dots
- Paper adhesive
- Computer with printer (optional)

Happy Anniversary Frame

Cut a 7⅞ x 7⅞-inch piece from lime green card stock. Using sewing needle and white thread, hand-stitch around outside edge of lime green square. Adhere to picture-frame insert.

Using 6½ x 6½-inch (#5) Grand Scalloped Squares die template, die-cut/emboss a scalloped square from printed paper. Adhere centered to lime green square.

Using Grand Squares die templates, die-cut/emboss a 5½ x 5½-inch (#4) square from black card stock and a 5 x 5-inch (#3) square from white card stock. Cut a photo down to 4¾ x 4¾ inches. Layer and adhere card-stock squares and photo as shown. Using foam squares, center and attach to scalloped square.

Tie a bow with ribbon; set aside.

Hand-print, or use a computer to generate, anniversary sentiment onto white card stock. Following Die Cutting Stamped Images instructions on page 4, die-cut/emboss sentiment using 1½ x 1½-inch (#2) Labels Sixteen die template. Chalk edges light brown. Punch a 3/16-inch hole through top of label and insert eyelet. Thread a length of white thread through eyelet, wrap around center of bow; tie knot. Trim ends. Adhere bow to bottom of photo as shown. Attach label in place using stacked foam squares.

Using 2⅜ x 2⅜-inch (#3), 1⅝ x 1⅝-inch (#2) and 1 x 1-inch (#1) Blossom Two die templates, die-cut/emboss flowers from white card stock for a total of three flowers. Score lines across flower petals to form dimensional petals. Chalk edges of flowers light brown. Layer and attach flowers to lower right corner of photo using adhesive dots. Thread button with cream string, tie knot in back. Trim ends. Attach to center of flower using adhesive dots.

Sources: *Card stock from WorldWin Papers; printed paper from 7gypsies; picture frame from North American Enclosures Inc.; die templates and Grand Calibur™ machine from Spellbinders™ Paper Arts.*

Materials

- 8 x 8-inch picture frame
- Card stock: black, lime green, white
- Avignon Decoration printed paper
- Light brown chalk
- 11 inches 11/16-inch-wide black/white stripe satin ribbon
- ⅛-inch silver eyelet
- Cream string
- White small button
- Black fine-tip marker
- Nestabilities die templates: Blossom Two (#S4-232), Labels Sixteen (#S4-301), Grand Squares (#LF-126), Grand Scalloped Squares (#LF-127)
- Grand Calibur™ manual die-cutting and embossing machine
- 3/16-inch hole punch
- Scoring tool
- Eyelet-setting tool
- Sewing needle and white thread
- Adhesive foam squares
- Adhesive dots
- Paper adhesive
- Computer with printer (optional)

Wedding Cake Display

Cover sides of all three box bottoms with printed paper. Wrap a strip of lime green card stock around each box lid.

Using Jumbo Scalloped Borderabilities Petite die template, die-cut/emboss enough white card stock to wrap over lime green strip on each box lid. Lightly chalk embossed areas with light brown. Adhere to top edge of each box lid.

Wrap a length of green grosgrain ribbon around top edge of each box lid as shown. Secure with adhesive.

Using Classic Scalloped Circles LG die templates, die-cut/emboss a 3⅝-inch (#5) scalloped circle from sage green card stock and a 4⅛-inch (#6) scalloped circle from white card stock. Layer and adhere scalloped circles to smallest box lid.

Using Grand Scalloped Circles die templates, die-cut/emboss a 4⅝-inch (#1) scalloped circle from sage green card stock

and a 5⅛-inch (#2) scalloped circle from white card stock. Layer and adhere scalloped circles to medium box lid.

Using Grand Scalloped Circles die templates, die-cut/emboss a 5⅝-inch (#3) scalloped circle from sage green card stock and a 6⅛-inch (#2) scalloped circle from white card stock. Layer and adhere scalloped circles to largest box lid. Stack and adhere boxes together as shown.

To create top flower, die-cut/emboss one of each of the following from white card stock using Blossom Two die templates: 1⅝ x 1⅝-inch (#2), 2⅜ x 2⅜-inch (#3), 3⅛ x 3⅛-inch (#4) and 3¾ x 3¾-inch (#5). Score lines across flower petals to form dimensional petals; lightly chalk light brown. Layer flowers together, pierce a hole through center and insert brad. Adhere to top of smallest box as shown.

Spellbinders Nestabilities Basics & Beyond

Create two small flowers by die-cutting/embossing two of each of the following from white card stock using Blossom Two die templates: 1 x 1-inch (#1), 1⅝ x 1⅝-inch (#2) and 2⅜ x 2⅜-inch (#3). Score lines across flower petals to form dimensional petals; lightly chalk light brown. Layer flowers together to create two flowers; pierce a hole through center of each stack of flowers and insert brads. Attach flowers to boxes as shown.

Thread cream string through each button; tie knots on backs. Trim ends. Attach a button to center of each flower.

Tie a bow with black/white striped ribbon; trim ends and adhere to bottom edge of smallest box. Attach acrylic stones around green ribbon as desired. ■

Sources: Papier-mache round-box set from CreateForLess; card stock from WorldWin Papers; printed paper from 7gypsies; Dew Drops acrylic stones from The Robin's Nest; die templates and Grand Calibur machine from Spellbinders™ Paper Arts.

Materials

- Papier-mâché round-box set
- Card stock: black, lime green, sage green, white
- Avignon Decoration printed paper
- Light brown chalk
- Ribbon: 11 inches ¹¹⁄₁₆-inch-wide black/white striped satin, 49 inches ¼-inch-wide sage green grosgrain
- Cream string
- White buttons: 1 large, 2 small
- White pearlescent diamond-shaped acrylic stones
- 3 silver brads
- Nestabilities die templates: Blossom Two (#S4-232), Grand Scalloped Circles (#LF-124), Classic Scalloped Circles LG (S4-124)
- Jumbo Scalloped Borderabilities® Petite die templates (#S4-241)
- Grand Calibur manual die-cutting and embossing machine
- Paper piercer
- Scoring tool
- Adhesive foam squares
- Adhesive dots
- Paper adhesive

Love & Gratitude

DESIGNS BY **SHERRY CHEEVER**

Rose Pyramid Card

Form a 5½ x 5½-inch top-folded card from blue card stock.

Adhere a 3¾ x 5¼-inch piece of printed paper to left side of 5⅜ x 5⅜-inch piece of light tan card stock leaving a ¹⁄₁₆-border along top, bottom and left edges. Adhere a 1½ x 5¼-inch piece of different printed paper to right side of light tan square, leaving a ¹⁄₁₆-inch border along top, bottom and right edges. Machine-stitch around outer edges of printed papers.

Using a 2⅛ x 2¾-inch (#4) Classic Rectangles SM die template, die-cut/emboss a rectangle from blue/tan dot printed paper; ink edges light brown. Using 2⅜ x 3⅛-inch (#4) Classic Rectangles LG die template, die-cut/emboss a rectangle from light tan card stock. Layer and adhere rectangles. Machine-stitch around edge of blue/tan dot rectangle. Adhere to upper left side of layered square.

Following Reverse Stenciling instructions on page 6, ink Classic Lace Border Grand die template dark brown and die-cut/emboss a 1½ x 5½-inch piece of blue card stock. Adhere to right side of layered square covering paper seam as shown. Wrap ribbon horizontally around square; tie bow on left side; trim ends.

Following Pyramid-Image Technique instructions on page 8, create layered image piece from digital image. **Note:** *If desired, ink edges of die-cut pieces before layering.*

Adhere to card front as shown.

Sources: *Card stock from Neenah Paper Inc. and Stampin' Up!; Petite Paper Pad from Webster's Pages; digital image from Twisted Papers; ribbon from May Arts; die templates and Grand Calibur™ machine from Spellbinders™ Paper Arts.*

Materials

- Card stock: light tan, blue, white
- Petite Paper Pad 6 x 6 Triple Pack
- Victorian Botanical digital image
- Dye ink pads: light brown, dark brown
- 26 inches 1¼-inch-wide cream silk ribbon
- Nestabilities® die templates: Labels Eleven (#S4-246), Classic Rectangles SM (#S4-130), Classic Rectangles LG (#S4-132)
- Classic Lace Border Grand Borderabilities® die templates (#S7-014)
- Grand Calibur™ manual die-cutting and embossing machine
- Sewing machine with cream thread
- Adhesive foam tape
- Paper adhesive
- Computer with color printer

Light Tomorrow Frame

Using matte gel medium, adhere printed paper to sides and front of frame. Cut out frame opening using craft knife. Sand all edges; ink edges light brown and dark brown.

Stamp sentiment onto white card stock using black ink. Following Die Cutting Stamped Images instructions on page 4, die-cut/emboss sentiment using 2⅝ x 1⅝-inch (#3) Labels Eleven die template; ink edges light brown. Die-cut/emboss a 2⅞ x 2⅛-inch (#4) label from blue/tan dot printed paper; ink edges light brown. Layer and adhere labels as shown.

Cut a piece of printed paper large enough to fit frame opening. Adhere labels to printed-paper panel; place inside frame. Trim labels as needed to fit inside frame.

Using black ink, stamp leaves onto Grungeboard using black ink; cut out. Ink front and back of leaves green; curl leaves as desired.

Following Dimensional Flowers instructions on page 9, create a flower using printed paper and 2-inch (#3) Blossoms die template. Ink edges of each die-cut blossom purple before forming flower. Using gloss medium, adhere and layer flower and leaves to left side of frame as shown. ■

Sources: Card stock from Neenah Paper Inc.; Petite Paper Pad from Webster's Pages; Grungeboard, ink pads, matte gel medium and gloss medium from Ranger Industries Inc.; Light Tomorrow stamp from Rubber Soul Inc.; Ticket to Art stamp set from Stampers Anonymous; die templates from Spellbinders™ Paper Arts.

Materials

- 2 x 3-inch wooden frame
- White card stock
- Petite Paper Pad 6 x 6 Triple Pack
- Grungeboard™
- Stamps: Light Tomorrow, Ticket to Art set
- Dye ink pads: light brown, dark brown, green, purple
- Black archival ink pad
- Nestabilities die templates: Labels Eleven (#S4-246), Blossom (#S4-192)
- Manual die-cutting and embossing machine
- Sandpaper
- Craft knife
- Matte gel medium
- Clear gloss medium
- Paper adhesive

Light Tomorrow with today.
Elizabeth Barrett Browning

With Love

DESIGNS BY **STACEY CARON**

With Love Card

Form a 6 x 6-inch top-folded card from white card stock.

Cut a 5½ x 5½-inch square from printed paper, adhere to red card stock; trim a small border. Wrap ribbon horizontally around panel; secure ends to back. Adhere square to card front.

Stamp label and sentiment onto white card stock. Following Die Cutting Stamped Images on page 4, die-cut/emboss stamped area using 4⅛ x 2¾-inch (#4) Labels Ten die template. Adhere to black card stock; trim a small border. Attach red rhinestones to top and bottom of label as shown. Using foam squares, attach to card front as shown.

Sources: *Card stock from WorldWin Papers; printed paper and rhinestones from My Mind's Eye; stamp sets from Waltzingmouse Stamps; ribbon from Creative Impressions Inc.; die template from Spellbinders™ Paper Arts.*

Materials

- Card stock: white, red, black
- Lush Black Damask flocked printed paper
- Stamp sets: Fancy Phrases, Very Vintage Labels No. 10
- Black dye ink pad
- Red rhinestones
- 7½ inches ¹¹⁄₁₆-inch-wide red ribbon
- Labels Ten Nestabilities® die templates (#S5-022)
- Manual die-cutting and embossing machine
- Adhesive foam squares
- Paper adhesive

Materials

- Red card stock
- Floral stem
- Wooden floral pick
- Wire
- Clear Glimmer Mist
- Deckled Rectangles LG Nestabilities die templates (#S4-202)
- Manual die-cutting and embossing machine
- Floral tape

Rose

Following Making a Rose instructions on page 9, assemble rose.

Attach finished rose to floral stem with floral tape. Spray finished rose with Glimmer Mist.

Sources: *Card stock from WorldWin Papers; Glimmer Mist from Tattered Angels; die templates from Spellbinders™ Paper Arts.*

Materials

- White small jewelry box
- White card stock
- Printed papers: Lush Black Damask flocked, Shaken Not Stirred Roger
- Very Vintage Labels No. 10 stamp set
- Black dye ink pad
- Red rhinestones
- 11¾-inch 11⁄16-inch-wide red ribbon
- 10-inches 1½-inch-wide black lace
- Nestabilities die templates: Labels Ten (#S5-022), Long Classic Scalloped Rectangles LG (#S4-143)
- Manual die-cutting and embossing machine
- ³⁄16-inch hole punch
- Adhesive dots
- Paper adhesive

Ring Box

Cover box bottom and box lid with Damask paper.

Using 2⅛ x 4¾-inch (#3) Long Classic Scalloped Rectangles LG die template, die-cut/emboss two rectangles from Roger printed paper. Wrap rectangles box bottom sides as shown, securing ends inside box.

Stamp label onto white card stock. Following Die Cutting Stamped Images on page 4, die-cut/emboss label using 2 x 1¼-inch (#1) Labels Ten die template. Punch a ³⁄16-inch hole through stamped end of label. Embellish with red rhinestones.

With box closed, wrap lace around box; tie bow on top; V-notch ends. Wrap red ribbon over black lace; thread through hole in label; tie bow; V-notch ends.

Sources: Card stock from WorldWin Papers; Lush Black Damask printed paper and rhinestones from My Mind's Eye; Shaken Not Stirred Roger printed paper from Kaisercraft; stamp set from Waltzingmouse Stamps; die templates from Spellbinders™ Paper Arts.

Monogrammed Candle

Project note: *Do not leave lighted candle unattended as paper wrap could catch fire as candle burns down.*

Wrap a piece of Damask paper around candle; secure ends together.

Stamp desired monogram image onto white card stock. Die-cut/emboss stamped image following Die Cutting Stamped Images instructions on page 4, using Standard Circles LG 2⅜-inch (#4) die template. Embellish with rhinestones.

Using largest Fancy Tags die template, die-cut/emboss a tag from Roger paper.

Layer and adhere die cuts to candle as shown. ■

Sources: Card stock from WorldWin Papers; Lush Black Damask printed paper and rhinestones from My Mind's Eye; Shaken Not Stirred Roger printed paper from Kaisercraft; stamp sets from JustRite; ribbon from Creative Impressions Inc.; die templates from Spellbinders™ Paper Arts.

Materials

- White candle
- White card stock
- Printed papers: Lush Black Damask flocked, Shaken Not Stirred Roger
- Deluxe Round Monogram Kit stamp set
- Black dye ink pad
- Red rhinestones
- Standard Circles LG Nestabilities die templates (#S4-114)
- Fancy Tags Shapeabilities® die templates (#S4-235)
- Manual die-cutting and embossing machine
- Adhesive foam squares
- Paper adhesive

Stamped Silhouettes

DESIGNS BY **GINA KRUPSKY**

So Very Sorry Card

Form a 4¼ x 4¼-inch top-folded card from gold card stock.

Using Butterflies embossing template, emboss a 3⅞ x 3⅞-inch piece of olive green card stock. Adhere to red card stock; trim a small border. Adhere to card front.

Cut a 2½ x 4½-inch piece from ivory card stock. Using foam blending tool, apply brown ink onto rectangle, dragging foam directly down piece. Stamp flower centered on inked rectangle with red ink. Following Die Cutting Stamped Images instructions on page 4, die-cut/emboss stamped area with 1⅝ x 3½-inch (#3) Long Classic Rectangles SM die template. Following Using Die Templates As Stencils instructions on page 6, ink outer edges of die-cut piece light brown using foam blending tool; remove die template. Adhere rectangle to right side of card front as shown.

Using dark brown ink, stamp sentiment onto a 2½ x 4½-inch piece of ivory card stock. Tear off top and bottom edges; ink torn edges light brown. Adhere to card front 1 inch above bottom edge.

Attach nailheads below sentiment as shown.

Sources: *Card stock and stamp set from Gina K. Designs; foam blending tool from Ranger Industries Inc.; nailheads from Mark Richards Enterprises Inc.; die templates and embossing template from Spellbinders™ Paper Arts.*

Materials

- Card stock: gold, red, olive green, ivory
- Botanicals stamp set
- Dye ink pads: brown, light brown, dark brown, red, olive green
- 5 (3mm) gold nailheads
- Long Classic Rectangles SM Nestabilities® die templates (#S4-144)
- Butterflies Impressabilities™ embossing template (#I2-1002)
- Manual die-cutting and embossing machine
- Foam blending tool
- Paper adhesive

Miss You Card

Form a 4¼ x 5½-inch top-folded card from olive green card stock.

Emboss a 3⅞ x 5⅛-inch piece of red card stock with Flourish embossing template. Ink embossed panel using foam blending tool and red ink. Adhere to gold card stock; trim a small border. Wrap ribbon horizontally around layered rectangle; secure ends to back. Adhere to card front.

Using light brown dye ink, stamp script background onto ivory card stock. Using red dye ink, stamp flower over script.

Following Die Cutting Stamped Images instructions on page 4, die-cut/ emboss stamped area with 1⅝ x 3½-inch (#3) Long Classic Rectangles

Materials

- Card stock: gold, red, olive green, ivory
- Botanicals stamp set
- Dye ink pads: brown, light brown, red
- 5 (3mm) gold nailheads
- 6 inches ⅝-inch-wide olive green stitched ribbon
- Nestabilities die templates: Long Classic Rectangles SM, (#S4-144), Long Classic Scalloped Rectangles SM (#S4-145), Standard Circles LG (#S4-114)
- Flourish Impressabilities embossing template (#I2-1009)
- Manual die-cutting and embossing machine
- Foam blending tool
- Adhesive foam dots
- Paper adhesive

SM die template. Following Using Die Templates as Stencils instructions on page 6, ink outer edges of die-cut piece light brown using foam blending tool; remove die template.

Using 1⅞ x 3¾-inch (#3) Long Classic Scalloped Rectangle SM die template, die-cut a scalloped rectangle from olive green card stock. Adhere stamped rectangle to scalloped rectangle.

Using 1⅝ x 3½-inch (#3) Classic Rectangles SM die template, die-cut a rectangle from gold card stock. Cut rectangle in half at an angle from lower right corner to upper left corner. Adhere pieces of rectangle to back of scalloped rectangle as shown.

Using brown ink, stamp "miss you" onto ivory card stock. In the same manner as before, die-cut/emboss sentiment using 1⅜-inch (#2) Standard Circles LG die template. Leaving die template in place, ink sentiment circle brown in the same manner as before. Adhere sentiment circle to right side of image panel as shown.

Using foam dots, attach image panel to card front as shown. Attach five nailheads to lower right corner of card front.

Sources: Card stock and stamp set from Gina K. Designs; foam blending tool from Ranger Industries Inc.; nailheads from Mark Richards Enterprises Inc.; die templates and embossing template from Spellbinders™ Paper Arts.

Thank You Card

Form a 5½ x 4¼-inch top-folded card from olive green card stock.

Using Flower Silhouette embossing template, emboss a 5⅛ x 4-inch piece of gold card stock. Ink embossed piece light brown using foam blending tool. Adhere to ivory card stock; trim a small border. Wrap ribbon horizontally around embossed panel; secure ends to back. Adhere to card front.

Using red ink, stamp flowers onto ivory card stock. Create lighter stamped images by stamping onto scrap paper before stamping onto ivory card stock. Using brown ink, stamp sentiment above flowers.

Following Die Cutting Stamped Images instructions on page 4, die-cut/emboss stamped area with 3¾ x 2⅞-inch (#5) Classic Rectangles LG die template. Following Using Die Templates As Stencils instructions on page 6, ink outer edges of die-cut piece light brown using foam blending tool; remove die template.

Die-cut a 4 x 3¼-inch (#5) Classic Scalloped Rectangles LG from red card stock. Adhere stamped rectangle to scalloped rectangle. Using foam dots, attach to card front as shown. Attach five nailheads next to lower right side of panel. ■

Sources: Card stock and stamp set from Gina K. Designs; foam blending tool from Ranger Industries Inc.; nailheads from Mark Richards Enterprises Inc.; die templates and embossing template from Spellbinders™ Paper Arts.

Materials

- Card stock: gold, red, olive green, ivory
- Scrap paper
- Botanicals stamp set
- Dye ink pads: brown, light brown, red
- 5 (3mm) gold nailheads
- 7 inches ⅝-inch-wide olive green stitched ribbon
- Nestabilities die templates: Classic Rectangles LG (#S4-132), Classic Scalloped Rectangles LG (#S4-133)
- Flower Silhouette Impressabilities embossing template (#I2-1015)
- Manual die-cutting and embossing machine
- Foam blending tool
- Adhesive foam dots
- Paper adhesive

miss you

thank you
for being such a good friend

so very sorry
thoughts and prayers are with you

DESIGNERS

Stacey Caron
www.spellbinderspaperarts.com/blog

Sherry Cheever
www.sherrycheever.blogs.
 splitcoaststampers.com

Kazan Clark
www.nunutoolies.blogspot.com

Kimberly Crawford
www.kimberly-crawford.blogspot.com

Linda Duke
www.lindaduke.typepad.com

Becca Feeken
www.amazingpapergrace.com

Terre Fry
www.terresscraptherapy.blogspot.com

Julie Gail
www.juliemcguffee.blogspot.com

Judy Hayes
www.judyhayesdesign.blogspot.com

Gina Krupsky
www.stamptv.ning.com

Ashley Cannon Newell
www.ashleynewell.blogspot.com

Julie Overby
www.joverby.blogspot.com

Debbie Seyer
www.debbieseyer.com

Holly Simoni
www.hollysimoni.typepad.com

Mary Snyder
e-mail: obsessedcropper1@typepad.com

BUYER'S GUIDE

7gypsies
(877) 412-7467
www.sevengypsies.com

A Muse Art Stamps
(877) 783-4882
www.amuseartstamps.com

American Crafts Inc.
(801) 226-0747
www.americancrafts.com

Bazzill Basics Paper Inc.
(800) 560-1610
www.bazzillbasics.com

Clearsnap Inc.
(888) 448-4862
www.clearsnap.com

Core'dinations
www.coredinations.com

Cosmo Cricket
(800) 852-8810
www.cosmocricket.com

Crafty Secrets Publications
(888) 597-8898
www.craftysecrets.com

CreateForLess
(866) 333-4463
www.createforless.com

Creative Impressions Inc.
(719) 596-4860
www.creativeimpressions.com

Fancy Pants Designs
(801) 779-3212
www.fancypantsdesigns.com

Fiskars
(866) 348-5661
www.fiskarscrafts.com

Gina K. Designs
(608) 579-1026
www.ginakdesigns.com

Graphic 45
(866) 573-4806
www.g45papers.com

Hero Arts Inc.
(800) 822-4376
www.heroarts.com

Imagination International Inc.
(541) 684-0013
www.copicmarker.com

Jenni Bowlin Studio
www.jbsmercantile.com

JustRite
www.justritestampers.com

Kaisercraft
(888) 684-7147
www.kaisercraft.net

Little Yellow Bicycle/The C-Thru Ruler Co.
(860) 290-2584
www.mylyb.com

Making Memories
(800) 286-5263
www.makingmemories.com

Mark Richards Enterprises Inc.
(888) 901-0091
www.markrichardsusa.com

May Arts
(203) 637-8366
www.mayarts.com

Maya Road
www.mayaroad.com

Michael Miller Fabrics
(212) 704-0774
www.michaelmillerfabrics.com

Michaels Stores Inc.
(800) MICHAELS (642-4235)
www.michaels.com

My Mind's Eye
(800) 665-5116
www.mymindseye.com

Neenah Paper Inc.
(800) 994-5993
www.neenahpaper.com

North American Enclosures Inc.
(800) 645-9209
www.naeframes.com

October Afternoon
(866) 513-5553
www.octoberafternoon.com

Papertrey Ink
www.papertreyink.com

Pink Paislee
(816) 729-6124
www.pinkpaislee.com

Pink Persimmon
(707) 695-9863
www.pinkpersimmon.com

Quietfire Design
www.quietfiredesign.ca

Ranger Industries Inc.
(732) 389-3535
www.rangerink.com

The Robin's Nest
(435) 789-5387
www.robinsnest-scrap.com

Rubber Soul Inc.
(360) 779-7757
www.rubbersoul.com

Spellbinders™ Paper Arts
(888) 547-0400
www.spellbinderspaperarts.com

Stampers Anonymous
(800) 945-3980
www.stampersanonymous.com

Stampin' Up!
(800) STAMP UP (782-6787)
www.stampinup.com

Tattered Angels
(970) 622-9444
www.mytatteredangels.com

Tsukineko LLC
(800) 769-6633
www.tsukineko.com

Twisted Papers
www.twistedpapers.com

Waltzingmouse Stamps
www.waltzingmousestamps.com

Webster's Pages
(800) 543-6104
www.websterspages.com

WorldWin Papers
www.worldwinpapers.com

The Buyer's Guide listings are provided as a service to our readers and should not be considered an endorsement from this publication.